*To Jack,*

# Greatness Thrust Upon Them

## NON-PROFESSIONAL ACTORS AND DIRECTORS
## DISCUSS THEIR ENCOUNTERS WITH SHAKESPEARE

*James F. Broderick*

Every Writer should have The
Experience of working with AN EDITOR
Like you once.

Once.

*Jim*

# Table of Contents

# Preface

As a freshman high school student in English class in 1977, I learned Shakespeare was born April 23, 1564. Over the course of this past year, as I interviewed actors, directors, and teachers across America, I learned that Shakespeare remains very much alive today. In fact, at this very moment, somewhere in a musty church basement, a mosquito-ridden public park, or an echo-filled school auditorium a troupe of players struggles with language that is five centuries old as they gingerly pull on a pair of tights, or walk through a carefully choreographed sword fighting scene. At any given moment on any day in America, an amateur actor is cloistered in his or her bedroom, den, basement, or car, reciting lines to himself or herself – a rewarding, agonizing process all actors must go through, and one that can be particularly prickly with Shakespeare.

Why do they do it? Why would busy, stressed-out adults or sleep-deprived students struggling just to keep up with the day-to-day demands of living and working willingly add to their over-stuffed in-boxes by piling on such a daunting additional demand on their time and intellect? What is it about this one playwright, a theatrical ghost whose work is often bequeathed to each generation under the heavy yoke of obligation, that makes factory workers, executives, teachers, computer programmers, and temp workers forsake a quiet evening at home or the local pub for the arduous journey backwards in time and language?

For the professional actor, the rewards are perhaps obvious: money, prestige, an impressive credential on one's performance vitae. But what of the non-professional? Why would someone whose work life lies outside the theatre labor so intensely, act by act, scene by scene, line by line, often under the most challenging of circumstances?

That's the question that came to me as I stood sweating under a merciless mid-day sun, strangling in a lace collar and brocade tunic upon a scraggly patch of green-brown grass in Paterson, New Jersey in the summer of 2012, waiting to make my entrance as Gonzalo in Shakespeare's *The Tempest*. Nervous, hot, worn down by a week of late-night rehearsals, and anxious about forgetting my lines in the only Shakespeare play I've been foolish enough to attempt, my first thought was "What the hell am I *doing?*" My next thought – as I looked around at Steve the dentist practicing his swordsmanship and Theresa the speech pathologist slipping into her fairy wings and Andy the high school student adjusting the tilt of his feathered hat and John the information technology special-ist smearing greasepaint on his cheeks — was why the hell are *they* doing this? I had come to know them all well enough to discover they each had a rich, full life. So why are they here, waiting for a cue, soon to enter amid an audience of no more than a dozen on-lookers on this humid, late-summer New Jersey afternoon? What, precisely, is *wrong* with these people?

What I discovered over the next year-and-a-half fills this book, and is a testament to what is *right* with these people, the passion-ate, committed, creative, literate, and thoughtful corps of actors who feel a kinship, however close or distant, with the colossus of English poetry and drama. I made many surprising discoveries in my conversations with these amateur actors, not the least of which was a change in my understanding of what "amateur" often really means. Many of the performers whose thoughts fill the following pages are, technically speaking, "amateurs." That is, most of them get little or no financial compensation for their work, whether act-ing or directing. Almost none of them make enough to quit their day jobs, as the cliché goes. But in terms of ability and training, their efforts are anything but amateur. I discovered that in even in the most modest and ad-hoc venues for Shakespearean performance, there is likely to be a resident thespian or two who *really* knows Shakespeare, has performed on professional stages and studied and perhaps even taught Shakespeare. Shakespeare the playwright draws smart and interesting people like Shakespeare in the park draws mosquitoes and high humidity.

To make matters even more interesting, this wide range of Shakespearean skill is often represented within any single troupe. That is, if you take in a "community theatre" production of Shakespeare, or catch a play under the canopy of a summer stage, or under the stars of a night-time amphitheatre performance, chances are you're seeing some actors who have never performed his works and others who quite possibly have performed at esteemed national theatre festivals, or with established Shakespeare companies, or even on film. And there they are, all together, each struggling to bring those words to life in that moment, to make the characters fresh and immediate and the language familiar in its strangeness.

So that's who I talked to for this book, a corps of talented people who spend their days selling insurance or solving computer problems or going to college or teaching elementary school or devising marketing campaigns or enjoying an active retirement. Some of them have found a way to incorporate their love of Shakespeare more completely into their work lives, serving as artistic directors and choreographers and college professors. Each of them has taken a different path. Many of the "non-professional" performers I interviewed for this book have studied Shakespeare seriously in college, or graduate school. Some have studied acting in some of the finest programs in the country. Others have had a more private relationship with Shakespeare – or sometimes no relationship at all. In the following pages – and on stages across the country – you'll find a breadth and depth of training and life experience that leads to an often thrilling alchemy, both for the performers on stage and the audiences that still seek out and support this profoundly affecting art.

"What was your first encounter with Shakespeare?" That question, or some slight variation of it, begins almost all the interviews in this book – a seemingly common starting point for a disparate world of responses and journeys. And amid the discursive and diverting anecdotes that shape the life of the performer (and the body of this book), we get closer to an answer to the question I kept thinking about on that scorching afternoon in Paterson. Or rather, we get closer to lots of answers, none any more alike than any two performances of *Hamlet*, or *A Midsummer Night's Dream*, or *The Tempest* could ever be. Part of Shakespeare's appeal is likely his mutability. No two Shakespeare performances are ever identical. In his variety lies a goodly measure of his singularity. And the passion, power, and persistence of his interpreters make clear, generation after generation, the greatness of his art.

Allow me to end on a personal note before completely retreating into the interrogator's guise: It was a genuine pleasure and a remarkably satisfying experience to be able to converse with such a vastly gifted and profoundly interesting group of people, from California to New York, from Alabama to North Dakota, from Ohio to Hawaii, from students just beginning their exploration of these works to more seasoned veterans of life's stages. Many of these interviews were initiated simply by "cold calls" I was making from names and phone numbers lifted from various theatrical directories. The actors who speak in the pages of this book were, to a person, unbelievably generous with their time, insights, and patience. I'm grateful to have crossed paths with each of them, and should I continue my personal quixotic attempt to perform Shakespeare again, I will take something from each of these humane and talented souls. My sincerest thanks to all the interviewees – and to you, dear reader, for joining in a journey that stretches back half a millennium and happily shows no sign of stopping.

# Angela Liao

*** I feel very alive when I
perform. When you're on
stage with other actors,
everything is a moment-to-
moment interaction.***

*Angela Liao has worked on numerous Shakespearean and contemporary
productions, the three most recent of which were with Hudson Shakespeare
Company in Northern New Jersey. Favorite roles have included Juliet in
Romeo and Juliet and Brutus in Julius Caesar.*

*In addition to theatre, Angela works on short film projects with Kevin
Chew, her husband and father of her beautiful girls, Sienna and Skylar.
She has been featured in print, commercial, industrial and film work.*

Q: DO YOU REMEMBER WHAT YOUR FIRST ENCOUNTER WITH
SHAKESPEARE WAS?

A: I think my first literal encounter was probably in English
class. I think we read *Julius Caesar.* I think we might have also read
*Romeo and Juliet.* This is probably high school, maybe ninth grade?
I think also in English class or creative writing, probably we read
some sonnets. I don't think I had that much appreciation for it – I

1

found it difficult, and I probably was one of those kids who needed the footnote version to figure out what they were actually saying.

Q: ACTING HAS BEEN A BIG PART OF YOUR LIFE SO FAR. DID YOUR INTEREST IN ACTING BEGIN IN HIGH SCHOOL? DID THEY HAVE A DRAMA CLUB — AND WERE YOU ACTIVE?

A: They had a drama club, and I remember auditioning for things, but I didn't get into anything. Basically, at that point, I didn't know what I was doing, and I didn't have "natural talent" or something, I don't know. But growing up in East Brunswick [New Jersey], there was a local dance-theatre school, so I went there, and took jazz classes and acting classes. It wasn't really until college, when I took an Acting 101 course, that I really loved it. It was so much fun.

Q: WHAT WAS YOUR FIRST EXPERIENCE PERFORMING SHAKESPEARE?

A: In college, my first play ever was *Winter's Tale*, and I played the shepherd's son, kind of a buffoonish character. That was through a Cornell theatre group.

Q: TELL ME ABOUT THAT PRODUCTION.

A: It was so much fun…I was still new to acting, and I didn't fully know what I was doing, but it was really fun because it was so physical. There's this one scene where he's talking about a ship-wreck, and the director was like "Go here, go there, show us! And remember all these big, dramatic arm movements while you're running around the stage!" It was just a lot of fun because on a

2

day-to-day basis you don't go around doing things like that, so it really stretches you.

Q: AND THEN YOU DID *ROMEO AND JULIET?*

A: In college, I played the apothecary, but also lots of little roles in the background. But that was fun because the director was like, "Think about it this way – this guy has been around drugs his whole life, so he'd probably be a little messed up," so I just had fun with it. It was almost like playing someone who was a drug addict, which was kind of an interesting interpretation. There's not much in the stage directions that say how to play that scene. It's a transactional scene, but at the same time, you say to yourself, why not try it this way?

Q: YOU PLAYED BRUTUS IN *JULIUS CAESAR* FOR THE HUDSON SHAKESPEARE COMPANY. DID YOU AUDITION FOR THAT PARTICULAR ROLE?

A: I did. That was my first lead role. Once I landed that lead, that first Shakespearean lead, I was proud of myself, but I also feel like a character is still a character, whether that character is briefly on stage, or on stage for the duration of the play. You still have to do your leg work. I don't know. I guess I'm saying it was not quite as drastic a leap as I would have imagined.

Q: BUT THERE'S A LOT MORE MEMORIZATION – SO HOW DID YOU PREPARE FOR BRUTUS?

A: In terms of the play itself, Jon [Ciccarelli, the director] gave us resources to do research on the play, the history, the background. In terms of memorization, I have my own process, and it's a process that works for me, where basically I'll tape record just my lines, and I try to read it deadpan, with no inflections, because I don't want my interpretation to be affected by some weird way I might have read the lines. So I'll just read the dialogue. And then I have another version where I record the cues, so if someone says to me "Come to the fire," then I'll record that and then leave some space so that when I'm practicing, I can say what I need to say. It helps me remember to hear the lines, as well as read them. Sight and sound. I'm pretty meticulous about the words because someone wrote this to be read a certain way, and even a little tiny thing such as a preposition, "to" instead of "from," it's still there, every word is important, and I try to be dead on.

Q: IS THE PROCESS YOU GO THROUGH PREPARING FOR SHAKESPEARE DIFFERENT FROM THE PROCESS YOU'D GO THROUGH PREPARING FOR A MORE MODERN WORK?

A: I would definitely say yes, because the language is so rich. It's not our common speech. The text is really like a puzzle, so a lot of times, when I read, you know, the dialogue, I'll usually highlight, or circle words and look them up in my lexicon, and I just take a lot of notes, and take it all in. It's like dissecting what's written.

Q: ARE YOU THE KIND OF ACTOR WHO LIKES TO SELF-DIRECT? OR WHEN YOU GO INTO THE REHEARSAL PROCESS, ARE YOU DESIROUS OF GETTING A DIRECTOR'S INPUT?

A: It's a collaborative process. I'm open to direction, and I don't propose to know what the director knows…they're trying to achieve a certain vision, and they have to keep in mind the whole play. But if I disagree with a director I'll speak up.

Q: YOU PLAYED JULIET – WHAT DID YOU DISCOVER ABOUT HER CHARACTER?

A: Everything is new to her. She's just discovering her world, just starting to come into her own and discovering the intensity of first love. That's really powerful. And the fact that she's going from childhood to adulthood within the span of two, three hours, that's just amazing. I really enjoyed that character.

In playing the role, I feel like the underlying want, or sexual desire, that's in the play has not always been clear. Reading off the page in high school, you don't realize as much that the language is kind of saying that. You might pick up on the innuendo, but as an adult, you hear that language and go "Oh….*that's* what she's saying." It's kind of eye-opening.

Q: DO YOU HAVE ANY ASPIRATIONS TO DIRECT?

A: No! (Laughs). I'm not sure I have the insights to discover all the nuances of the play. Certainly not a Shakespeare play – maybe something more modern. I'd have to get my feet wet.

Q: ANY SHAKESPEARE ROLES YOU'D LIKE TO PERFORM THAT YOU HAVEN'T YET?

A: I think maybe Lady M. Or one of the witches, because I think that sounds like so much fun. Maybe people are drawn to roles that that are not like themselves – or facets of themselves that others don't see. So I think in "real life," no one would picture me as Lady M, but I think that would be interesting to play.

Q: DO YOU THINK YOUR ETHNICITY HAS HAD AN IMPACT ON YOUR ABILITY TO GET ROLES IN SHAKESPEARE PLAYS? AND DO YOU THINK ASIAN ACTORS FACE ANY KINDS OF OBSTACLES WHEN SEEKING ROLES IN SHAKESPEARE PLAYS -- OR IN THE THEATRE IN GENERAL?

A: I think my ethnicity hasn't been a barrier when it comes to being cast in Shakespeare plays. Since his work has been around for so long, there have been countless examples of directors taking risks with his work, and casting non-traditionally in terms of race and gender. People are not as surprised when they see "ethnic" actors playing traditionally "Caucasian" roles in Shakespeare's plays.

Q: YOU HAVE HAD A VARIED ACTING CAREER. WHAT IS IT YOU GET FROM PERFORMING?

A: I feel very alive when I perform. When you're on stage with other actors, everything is a moment-to-moment interaction. It's just that you don't know what is going to happen next. You say the lines, but you don't know how the other actor is going to react that particular day, that particular second, and of course, there's the audience. They are part of that community, that energy at that point in time. They're reacting to what's going on, sometimes silently – but you can *feel* that.

# Rick Kenney

*" We usually don't do it [teach Shakespeare] in this country until high school, but I think we need to start a few years earlier. It's a better time to get their interest."*

*Rick Kenney is a retired government public affairs officer and second-career teacher who lives in Reston, Virginia. He first found the fun in Shakespeare as an undergraduate drama major at Catholic University in Washington, DC. Then, during his working years, he kept an active interest on the side by participating in community theatre. Between 1970 and 2002, when he retired from Civil Service, he worked in 48 different theatrical productions, including six Shakespeare plays.*

*In retirement, he became a middle school drama and English teacher and introduced Shakespeare to his students by co-directing A Midsummer Night's Dream and adapting his own script of The Taming of the Shrew for another student production. His classroom and stage experience led him to postgraduate studies at The Shakespeare Institute (University of Birmingham) in Stratford-upon-Avon, England, where he earned an MA in Shakespeare and Education in December 2011, and performed with the Institute Players, playing Andrew Aguecheek in Twelfth Night, Leonato in Much Ado About Nothing, and Shylock in The Merchant of Venice.*

Q: What was your first encounter with Shakespeare?

A: The best memory of my first encounter was in the classroom as an undergraduate in college. I think we must have read at least one play in high school – don't remember what it was. When I got to college [Catholic University] – I had choices for English electives. I chose Shakespeare, largely because of the drama connection. I had this excellent professor – Frank Maguire. He didn't have his Ph.D., but he was such an excellent teacher he had a waiting list. The fist week, he had a participatory reading, almost like a director casting a play. He gave us parts – it was *Henry IV, Part One*. Sitting there, listening to my classmates read – he didn't pick me first – and then he called on me to read King Henry. It was just a small scene, and as I was reading it, after having listened to other classmates tell the story, I really started feeling this character of the dad who's disappointed in his son. I can remember what was going on, what building we were in, what classroom. Probably, because I've been studying Shakespeare the last few years, it's even clearer now.

Q: Why do you think that memory is so vivid?

A: It was personal to me. There might be others who remember that – the students idolized him. He really got you into the subject. What really struck me was the difference between listening and saying the lines, you know, just reading it as they do in most classrooms. But we were reading it like actors, like you would do in the first week of a production. You get such a better feel for what's going on. And it came from my drama training – I had done a lot of plays in high school, but had never done any Shakespeare. This really lit up my drama instincts.

10

Q: Were you active in theatre throughout college?

A: I did audition for the school plays – got into two of them. We also did a lot of workshops. I got into an original musical about congress. Then I did Brecht, I think it was. It wasn't a very memorable experience. I had a bit part – most of the performing was done by grad students. Most of the performing I did was back home, in the summer time. I did a lot of musicals with my high school – they called it the alumni production, though there were kids in the high school who were also in it. I played the King in *The King and I*, one of the barbershop quartet in *Music Man*, and Merlin in *Camelot*.

Q: Did you want to be an actor?

A: No – in fact, the director we had in high school persuaded us you didn't have to think about acting as a career, it was something you could always do, apart from your career. I didn't think I wanted to go to New York, and the grind of going on auditions all the time. Then when I got to Catholic University, in the drama program, they took the approach that the way you become a good performer, actor, theatre person, is to learn a lot about life, the world, everything that matters to human beings. The technical stuff you can learn on the job. The emphasis wasn't on the craft, but absorbing as much as you can about life. It was the liberal arts approach – drama for its own sake, not to prepare for a career, but to enrich your own life. We were told to be a true `amateur' – do it for the love of it.

But one of my classmates was Susan Sarandon. She really had ambitions to do professional acting. She was a model, and I guess she had lots of contacts. She really got into it right after college.

In the 1960s, we still had a draft, and the Vietnam war was raging, and they had a good ROTC program on campus, and I talked with my dad, and he said it probably would make sense, go into the Air Force, you'll have a job. So I graduated, got my commission – and went into the Air Force, but not in public information right away. They made me what is called a weapons controller – an officer who directs aircraft. I did that for 18 months, and once I served an overseas assignment, I got diverted to Taiwan. When I got back, I applied for and got training for public information.

Q: SO YOU HAD TO PUT YOUR ACTING ON HOLD?

A: Not exactly. I was in Plattsburgh, and I found a group there that put shows on and joined them. My wife, who I met at Catholic University, also had an interest in acting, so we tried to stay involved. We had a daughter at the time, so that was a bit of a distraction. But I stayed active – this was the big message I got from Father Hartke [Rev. Gilbert V. Hartke, a Dominican priest who established the Department of Speech and Drama at Catholic University in 1937 and headed it until 1974]. This is something you can do all the time. And the idea I got from Frank Maguire: All the world's a stage, and we're all playing roles every day. I definitely saw this in my job as a public information officer, and in helping others with their role playing. This gets philosophical, but drama is a life skill. I might not have articulated it that way at that time, but I knew I wanted to continue performing, becoming different characters.

Q: AND YOU CONTINUED TO FOCUS ON SHAKESPEARE – WHY?

A: I have to go back to that discovery in Frank Maguire's class – there has always been something about Shakespeare that thrills me more than other playwrights. Think about him just as a playwright: you get into his plays, you have to work for it, it's not something that comes easily. The more you discover, the more you want to discover. I think I began – it goes back to 1999 – when I offered to direct *The Taming of the Shrew* for the Elden Street Players [of Herndon, Virginia]. I had been in several productions of Shakespeare's plays, *Twelfth Night, As You Like It, Antony and Cleopatra*. I kept offering to direct a Shakespeare play to get them interested. In 1996, I played Prospero in *The Tempest*, the ghost and player king in *Hamlet*. I finally got my chance in 1999. I directed *The Taming of the Shrew*. It was that that forced me to do a really close reading of the text, and figure out how to adapt it for amateur performance, and make it fun and funny for the audience. I didn't want to take on a controversial interpretation, or a feminist deconstruction, I saw the play as a comic love story, and wanted to get that across to the audience. A lot of people I talked to – especially females – said "I hate that play!" The whole politics of the play…there's more to it that I wanted to bring out. I edited the text, prepared a text for performance, and that really sold me on doing more and more of that. The more you get into it, the more you want to get deeper into it. It's magic. That's why there's no sign of interest in Shakespeare letting up. Right now I'm working on a text of *The Winter's Tale* for possible production.

Q: How did you end up attending the Shakespeare Institute?

A: Because I was retired, I went into teaching part-time, by choice, and I got to focus on what I really wanted to teach, which was drama. I was teaching two to three classes per semester, which was just right, plus the after-school rehearsals. I was really able to immerse myself in it, and I was really enjoying it, but because I was a part-time teacher taking care of drama, which was an elective, I was expendable. That's when I decided to go to the Shakespeare Institute – so I took a leave of absence.

The Shakespeare Institute is actually part of the University of Birmingham, which isn't far from Stratford-upon-Avon – working in concert with the RSC and the Shakespeare Birthplace Trust. I signed up for the Shakespeare in Education program. I saw that this is really the time [middle school] to start teaching Shakespeare. We usually don't do it in this country until high school, but I think we need to start a few years earlier. It's a better time to get their interest. I went into this program, already knowing what I wanted to do my research on: teaching Shakespeare in middle school, ages 11-14. There's a whole bunch of things you can use Shakespeare to teach. I already had the master's degree and they asked me if I wanted to go for the Ph.D., but that leads more into the academic analysis, and I wanted to focus on the practical applications. So I got another master's degree.

Q: WHAT DID YOU GET FROM THE PROGRAM?

A: You mean besides the degree? The sense of being there in Stratford was a palpable feeling – to walk the grounds of the gardens, and the streets of Stratford, past the Guild Chapel where Shakespeare probably attended services, and going through the house and the trappings of Shakespeare's life, going to see the plays at the Shakespeare Royal Theatre, was something that gave me tingles. You walk the graveyard outside Holy Trinity church, and you get that feeling. The place is haunted – in a good way. It really came to be real. But the best part of it was in performing the plays – we did *Twelfth Night*, and *Much Ado*, with other students. Performing Shakespeare with other actors who really love Shakespeare was the best experience I've ever had on stage.

# Meredith Zahn

**" *Everyone knows how brilliant Shakespeare was – I knew that from just watching, before I could even understand the words. But then when you perform it, you realize that no one can ever get to the bottom of it.* "**

*Meredith Zahn has been performing her entire life. She started doing shows on her family room coffee table at age 2, performing for anyone who would be her audience. At age 3 she started dance classes and was a competitive dancer for seven years. Meredith always enjoyed singing, too, and then tried her hand at musical theatre.*

*She continued to study dance, voice, and acting, while performing in 20+ theatre shows, two independent films, TV commercials, and as a singer. Recently, Meredith has begun writing her own music, too. After writing almost 100 songs, she has just released a professionally produced demo. Meredith is currently pursuing a Bachelor of Fine Arts in Musical Theatre at Wright State University in Dayton, Ohio.*

Q: You started taking dance classes at three, and you've continued performing ever since then. Is your desire to perform a family trait?

A: No one in my family performs at all! We've talked about this. My brother tried to play piano but it didn't work out. I had a great uncle who played music, but he's like the only one.

Q: So where does that come from?

A: I have a huge faith – Christian faith. I feel He gave me the gifts that I have to have the opportunity to be something that people can look up to. At every curtain call, I like to blow a kiss up to the sky. People ask me why, and I tell them that's my thanking God. Performing has given me a chance to share my testimony. I feel that God put me in this position.

In one show that I was in, I had to wear a mustache. I needed to roll up a bandaid to make it stick, and I was like, "Please Jesus let this mustache stick!" People after the show asked me "Why were you praying about your mustache?" Well, that gave me a chance to testify about my faith, which I was happy to do. I understand the theatre world is not always very religious – I get that, but it gives me a chance to share my faith with others, if they want to know.

Q: Were you active in theatre in school?

A: I was actually home schooled from second grade, but when I was twelve, and had been dancing for all those years, there was a summer program at Columbus Children's Theatre. They would hold auditions, and then you'd be part of a conservatory. After several more weeks of workshops, we were able to audition for other shows. I eventually decided to quit dance competitions so I'd have time to do shows all year round. I was afraid once I quit dance I'd never get cast – but that first year, I did nine shows in fourteen months!

Q: DID YOU FEEL PREPARED FOR THAT?

A: I think people underestimated just how much stage presence and comfort I had doing the dancing – I had been on stage from 3, 4, 5 years old. I felt like I was meant to be on stage. I always loved singing but acting was the one thing I had no experience with, although we had a little drama department – in a sort of co-op of other home-school students. There was a woman whose degree was in theatre. She taught the drama class. You didn't have to audition. We'd write our own scripts, and then we'd read through them, and vote on which we wanted to do. Normally, the seniors got first choice of what they wanted to do. We'd do different theatre games, we'd rehearse for about twelve weeks, and we'd have a showcase where we'd perform our half hour skits.

Q: WHAT WAS YOU FIRST ENCOUNTER WITH SHAKESPEARE?

A: In Schiller Park, in Columbus, they always put on these shows – Shakespeare in the Park. My mom took me when I was like nine, and I remember I hated it. I just didn't understand what was happening. It was so long – I just hated it. But then my mom made me go again – and I just tried to bear it. Then the next summer, I went again. And little by little, I started getting used to it, just blocking out the words and sort of just feeling what was happening between the actors. I just kind of watched it. And then I fell in love with it. Then, I decided I'd figure out how

19

the words work. We had a Shakespeare book, and I took it down, and read it. I was probably 11 or 12 – and it still didn't make a lot of sense to me.

Well, getting ready to go to college as a theatre major, I hadn't done any Shakespeare. I said, "Meredith, you've got to do this." I decided to audition for The Actors Theatre of Columbus. I signed up and my mother said, "You realize this is Shakespeare in the Park!" And I thought, "What am I doing? These people are like professionals." But I auditioned, and I got a call back. I really had no idea what I was saying. I said to a friend of mine in the hallway outside the audition, "Can you tell me what this even means?"

Q: HOW DID THE AUDITION GO?

A: Well, I remembered one thing my acting coach told me – just pick an objective and stick to it. So I picked one, went in, and did it. And then, after I did it, in front of all those people, it sounded so stupid to me. I remember sitting in my car, wanting to cry. I thought "Why am I even doing this?" And that's why I was stunned when, two weeks later, I got the email that said I had the part of Luciana in *A Comedy of Errors*.

A couple of weeks later, the director called me and I said "Do you have ANY books that can help me?" He told me about *No Fear Shakespeare*. That helped so much, going line by line through the whole play. I'm not a scared person, but I wasn't sure I could do this. But I did it. I worked with the *No Fear Shakespeare*, saying my lines over and over, trying to get comfortable.

I went to that first rehearsal and we did a cold read – Shakespeare plays are meant to be performed. As soon as I was with the other

20

actors, it all made sense to me. And I was like, "I get what I'm saying now! Oh my gosh, it makes sense."

Q: DID YOU ASK YOUR FELLOW CAST MEMBERS FOR ADVICE?

A: I was definitely that person that always said "How do you pronounce this?" or "Do I phrase these together or are they separate thoughts?" I was the baby in the cast, and so I asked everybody questions. Since Shakespeare is meant to be performed, the more I tried to *show* people what I was saying, the more it made sense to me. It's beautiful – Shakespeare is the best writer of all time. There are so many things he says in a gorgeous, unexpected way – it's just beautiful. There wasn't a time we ran through the show that I didn't discover something new in the play. I worked on that show for two months, and yet I never got tired of it. I don't know that I can say that about any other show I've done. It's a never-ending ocean of beautiful thoughts.

Everyone knows how brilliant Shakespeare was – I knew that from just watching, before I could even understand the words. But then when you perform it, you realize that no one can ever get to the bottom of it.

Q: WHAT DID PERFORMING SHAKESPEARE TEACH YOU ABOUT HIS WORKS?

A: Shakespeare made up words – he literally made them up. And he didn't always know how to use punctuation. There are mistakes everywhere. He doesn't know how to spell. In *A Comedy of Errors*, there are fart jokes – and I thought, this guy Shakespeare is maybe not as fancy as we think he is. I don't think he would want people to look at his work and say "I'll never get this."

Q: Do you think most people – especially younger people – feel that way about his work?

A: I think it's hard to force someone to do something they don't want to do. I was fortunate to have my experience with reading Shakespeare being something I wanted to do, even if I wasn't ready. If someone is going into reading it with a negative connotation, being forced to read it, that just won't work. If I were teaching it, I'd give my class an option: you read the Shakespeare play *you* want to read. Not everyone relates to *Romeo and Juliet*. Most people might not ever relate to it. But if you can pick something that relates to you, what you are interested in, you'll care a little more.

Q: When did you make the decision to pursue performing seriously?

A: I think I always knew I was meant to perform – I wasn't always sure I wanted to study it. I used to think I'd be a business major. But then I realized there is so much further that I can go into what I love to do. And these days, tons of people are performing. Anyone can sing – you need to have a leg up on people. And the study of Shakespeare performance is never ending. Creativity is like, the more you use, the more you have.

I'm going into this – and I'm trusting God. I believe God's plan is for me to go to Wright State and get a degree, and then go to New York. I have to try – even if I'm not meant to do theatre, I feel like I couldn't go and be a housewife, or a personal assistant, if I didn't at least try to do this, follow my passion, and just try. I have heard from other people about how they wish they had just tried! I will accept God's plan and go wherever he wants me to go, but I couldn't just stay here in Ohio wondering "What if...?"

Q: Your faith is obviously an important part of your life — your personal life and your performance life. Has it always been that way?

A: I grew up in a completely Christian household. But I wasn't personally saved and didn't develop a relationship with Jesus until about a year and a half ago. And that was really something – but I didn't want to be one of these people with a bullhorn announcing my faith. How do I develop the ability to tell people about God? What can I do? And the message I got was just to be a child of God. Go out and radiate the faith you feel, and people will ask you about your faith. It's little things, like when people say, "How are you?" I'll say, "I'm great – Jesus rocks!" And they'll be like, "What do you mean? Why did you say that?" And that opens a door.

Q: What are your professional aspirations?

A: I have the most outrageous dream role ever – before I die, I'd like to play Glinda in *Wicked*, and then play Elphaba in *Wicked*. I want to play them both. Lots of people have dreamed of doing one or the other, but I'd like to play both. I don't think there are very many people who could play Elphaba, and really connect on a deep level, and then also play Glinda at an equally deep level. I'd like to connect in that way. I'd enjoy digging in and finding those connections, looking into both Elphaba and Glinda. I'm not sure very many people would have the guts to do both. But I'd like to try.

# Dennis Brestensky

> **"** *We had to perform in a lecture hall. A nice lecture hall, but it wasn't designed for plays. Stage left was a hallway. Stage right was a wall.* **"**

*Dennis F. Brestensky, emeritus professor of English, received his M.A. in English from Duquesne University and doctorate in English education from West Virginia University. He taught introductory Shakespeare for non-majors for 42 years at Penn State Fayette, where he founded a Shakespeare festival and with his students, non-theatre majors, began The Lion Players, a student-directed theatre group committed to performing Shakespeare.*

*He has studied at the Folger Shakespeare Library, researching the teaching of Shakespeare, with special emphasis on master teachers and performance-based teaching of Shakespeare. He has made presentations on these topics at national conferences and conducted a survey to identify master Shakespeare teachers, publishing the results in Shakespeare and the Classroom. About one of these master teachers, he has published a book, The Teaching Legacy of O.B. Hardison, Jr. Other publications about teaching and literature appeared in English Journal, Modern Language Studies, and West Virginia Philological Quarterly.*

*Brestensky's honors include: Fayette Campus Teaching Excellence Award, Lindback Award for Distinguished Teaching, College of Liberal Arts Award for Outstanding Contribution to the Humanities, Outstanding Fellow of Fayette Campus, The Commonwealth College Outstanding Service to Students Award, and Fayette's Scholarly Excellence Award.*

Q: DO YOU REMEMBER YOUR FIRST EXPERIENCE WITH SHAKESPEARE? WAS IT A MOVIE? A LIVE PRODUCTION? OR WAS IT JUST THE WORDS ON THE PAGE?

A: It was on the page. It was *Julius Caesar*. It must have been my sophomore year. I wanted to be an English teacher then. It's so strange – most people wouldn't know what they wanted to do. There was this crazy thing in my head – there were not enough male English teachers, not enough guys who liked English. I guess maybe they thought it was sort of a "sissy" thing to get into. I thought as a guy I could get more males involved.

Q: DID YOU FIND SHAKESPEARE DIFFICULT AT FIRST?

A: We were all intimidated by it. There was a nun, I can't remember her name...she said exactly that: we're all intimidated by Shakespeare's language. For two reasons: it's old – the language, the allusions, the historical references are more than four hundred years old. Plus, it's poetry, and poetry can be tough. We had a hard time analyzing poems of four and eight lines. Some of these plays are eighty to ninety percent poetry. That helped me to be not so upset, to know that teachers still have to wrestle with the language.

But the thing I really liked about Shakespeare – he had a rounded vision of life. Some of the literature we were reading was

26

negative, but even though Shakespeare wrote tragedies, he had a great vision of the world, of the comedy and joy of life. You'd cry when you read his works, but you'd also laugh.

Q: WHAT WERE YOUR EXPERIENCES WITH SHAKESPEARE LIKE IN COLLEGE?

A: The Shakespeare courses weren't necessarily the most positive. I had to take this one priest, I remember. It wasn't a good course. When you took an exam, he never posted the grade. And he never gave you any feedback on papers. The myth on the campus was that he just got the papers from the English majors, and threw them on the steps. Whatever step they fell on, A, B, C, D, F, well that's what you got. You'd think that would have turned me off, but it didn't. He was very knowledgeable about Shakespeare, in class discussions, but it was odd he never commented on the papers.

Q: PRESUMABLY YOU GOT MORE FEEDBACK IN GRADUATE SCHOOL?

A: I was in a Ph.D. program in Pitt – I didn't like it. You had to give them back their ideas. If you did something original, they didn't like it. I was told about the program at West Virginia – a doctorate in education, an Ed.D., not a Ph.D. It was a program in Education with an emphasis in English. That suited me much better...I was introduced to Maslow's work, and my study of that informed the rest of my work. It's an experiential approach, and that's the approach I've taken with Shakespeare. That's the idea behind the Lion Players [a student-driven performance group at Penn State], using your life experiences to enhance your academic work.

Q: HOW DID THE LION PLAYERS GET STARTED?

A: Throughout the years I taught English 129, "Intro to Shakespeare." It was a gen ed course, a humanities elective. The students – not every time I taught it, but often – they'd say "Let's do a Shakespeare play." I always found ways to put it off. I never acted, never directed. Then in 1997 – about three decades later – about a half dozen students came into my office, closed the door, and said rather forcefully, "We want to do a Shakespeare play. We want to form a Shakespeare club called the Lion Players. We want to do a full-length play every spring, and we want you to be behind us. Not as director, but as advisor, supporter, and cheerleader." They wanted it to be student-centered. That was their idea. And that was very appealing to me. I had some experience with a student-centered approach. I was doing other student-centered activities when they came to me and said they wanted to succeed or fail on their own, and that they wanted me to sort of guide them, give them advice, maybe even bail them out. That sounded great to me. That's how it started.

Q: IT WASN'T JUST A PERFORMING GROUP, RIGHT? DIDN'T IT TURN INTO AN ACTUAL COLLEGE COURSE?

A: Well, I proposed it as a course, but didn't build in anything else, not any formal academic papers. The only requirement was just a journal where the students reflect on their experience. And the course got accepted. I required them to participate, of course, and we had books, and there were films we watched and discussed. But I told them I wouldn't grade the quality of their acting performance, and the only writing would be in their journals.

Q: What was the first year of the Lion Players like?

A: Very chaotic! We had no theatre dept, no theatre professors to help us with costumes, set design, all that stuff. We had no auditorium. We had to perform in a lecture hall. A nice lecture hall, but it wasn't designed for plays. Stage left was a hallway. Stage right was a wall. So we put a curtain along the back that you could hide behind.

Q: What was your first production?

A: We did *Romeo and Juliet*. When we got to know each other better, we held an election for director. Each person gave a little speech, what their interest was, what their experience was. Our first director was an adult student, which helped. That first year, we had a budget of about $500, and we worked with some engineering professors to help us build and design the sets. And we had some students from their classes who helped. Luckily, they had their own tools. Some of the local lumber yards would give us cheap lumber. The art professor would recommend people from his class who could paint the set. We had business majors join us who could do the marketing for the play. Because we had no theatre department, we had no structure in place. It became a very collaborative thing – it wasn't just the English dept.

And now, former Lion Players help out – it's been that way every year. Some years, we really lean on them to bail us out. If we lose somebody a couple of weeks before a performance, these people step in and learn a role in two weeks. We really count on them.

Q: HOW DO THE PERFORMANCES TURN OUT, USUALLY?

A: In general, the performance they end up doing at the end of this struggle through four months is so good, so uplifting, they match up against other college theatre departments – and I don't know how they do it. People will say: "How professionally done that show was! We didn't expect this to be done at such a high level." The really great productions that result from this student-centered collaborative effort are important, but what students learn from the process is really what's significant.

# John Bylancik

> *" It got to the point where it almost didn't matter if anybody was going to show up to watch it. Just being able to do this is really kind of cool. "*

*Born in Albany, NY at the dawn of the Space Age, John Bylancik's early years were full of wonder and imagination. Always happy to be, if not the center of attention, at least within the 10-point circle, this acting business is not a complete surprise. Other than participating in high school musicals, John never pursued any interest in studying, or actually doing, any acting after that. After nearly 35 drama-less years, it nonetheless was a wonder to friends and family why he got it into his imagination that he could, let alone should, try his hand at community theatre - and at Shakespeare no less! And yet, he did.*

[NOTE: I first met John Bylancik when we performed together in an amateur production of *The Tempest* in Montclair, New Jersey. I began my questioning with a comment about that experience]

Q: I FOUND IN YOUR FIRST READING A KIND OF ENTHUSIASM, AND A SURPRISINGLY UNSELFCONSCIOUS ENGAGEMENT WITH THE MATERIA. SO LET ME BEGIN BY ASKING YOU, WHAT EXPERIENCE

HAVE YOU HAD WITH SHAKESPEARE, EITHER AS A READER OR A PERFORMER? WHAT WAS YOUR RELATIONSHIP WITH SHAKESPEARE BEFORE THIS PLAY – AND WHAT WAS YOUR THEATRICAL EXPERIENCE?

A: High school musicals. It was somewhat fortuitous that the football tryouts and play tryouts were the same day, and I had to choose between the two. I was late for the football tryouts, and the coach shut the locker room door. It was like, "Hey, you're on time, or you're out." So I turned around and went to the auditorium – and I got a part. I was always one of those two sort-of "foible" characters in the background, you know, in every big musical there's always a Mutt and Jeff character. I was always Jeff. Spent four years being that character, and got hooked on it, really loved it. There's a little bit of theatre in my family. My dad was in community theatre right before he got drafted. A lot of cousins were involved, so as a family we were pretty regularly going to see somebody in something. It was like "Oh, Tony's in *Carousel* over in Schenectady, so let's go."

In college, I took a different route, never really got back to it.

Q: WHERE'D YOU GO TO COLLEGE?

A: SUNY Stony Brook out on Long Island. I went out there thinking I'd go into their clinical psych program. I spent three years running rats through mazes and I thought, "This is not what I want to do." So I became a business major there, got that bug. Wound up going to grad school for business. I've sort of had a sales and marketing business track ever since I got out. I was do-ing sales training, so I got comfortable in front of people, and I've worked in the technology sector where my job would be to explain the technology to new users, so I've never been shy. My dad was never really shy either. He was always pulling stunts at home.

Q: SO WHAT MADE YOU WANT TO GET BACK INTO THEATRE?

A: The only reason I said yes to *The Tempest* was I turned 50 last year, and I was sort of thinking about what I'd be doing my fiftieth year, and I decided I wanted to say yes to some different things. Just for a year, I was going to say yes to some things I normally wouldn't have.

Q: SO FATE PUT YOU THERE IN THAT PRODUCTION. TALK TO ME ABOUT WHAT YOUR LEVEL OF AWARENESS WAS ABOUT SHAKESPEARE. DO YOU REMEMBER READING HIM IN HIGH SCHOOL?

A: We went through a couple of plays in high school. I had a really good English teacher. We did some Shakespeare-Tolkien comparisons, which was interesting. I've always been a big Tolkien fan. And, since I've gone to work for the school [Montclair's Kimberley Academy,] I'm in a technology department, very removed from student work, but my kids were always involved. And the school's got a curriculum where in the middle school, you spend a year in a Shakespeare unit in English, history, and fine arts. So they're sort of immersed in Shakespeare in their seventh grade year. It features a student production every year where, because they've studied it from September to December, they start putting a production together in January, and they get to drive a lot of the interpretation and the creative elements of it. There's no teacher sitting there saying, "Read these lines this way," or "This is what this means, so perform it *this* way." I learned a lot just helping out, crewing those shows, really just watching Christian [director Christian Ely] help these kids through the process. Little things he said, like "Shakespeare happens at the speed of thought." That's one of the things he teaches. Shakespeare isn't slow, or laborious. It's just as fast as people having conversations as they are happening. Little bits and pieces I've heard him pass on. And then following Krissy [his daughter] through her love of acting brought us to tour the Globe Theatre in London. So it's always been very peripheral, something that belonged to someone else. But very interesting, nonetheless.

Q: DID YOU EVER HAVE IT IN YOUR HEAD THAT ONE DAY YOU WERE GOING TO SEEK OUT SOME OPPORTUNITIES TO PERFORM?

A: Oddly enough, if there was any of that, it was the thought that when I retire, if a local community theatre is doing a musical, maybe I'll try out. In the same realm as trout fishing, and all the other things I'm going to do when I retire, it would be on that list, with no real directed thought to it at all.

Q: LET'S TALK A LITTLE BIT ABOUT THE PROCESS OF PREPARING TO PLAY CALIBAN. WHEN YOU WERE CAST, DID YOU HAVE ANY SENSE OF THE COMPLEXITY OF THE ROLE?

A: (laughs) I couldn't even pronounce his name! I had to go online and find a recording where somebody spoke the character's name so I'd get that part right.

Q: SO YOU REALLY WERE STARTING FROM SCRATCH.

A: Oh yeah. And I had no idea that it was supposed to be the comedic center of the show, until way later. I think in an age before the internet, I might not have been able to pull it off, because of the hours I spent watching performances, watching online classes, where community college teachers would teach a unit on *The Tempest*, and I'd sit there and watch that. And I'd say "Oh God – *that's* what's going on there."

Q: CALIBAN IS A HIGHLY COMIC ROLE, BUT IT CAN ALSO BE VERY DARK.

A: The more I got into it, the more I was really glad I did, because of the complexity of it. All the descriptions of it refer to him as one of Shakespeare's larger-than-life characters who embodies earth and sky, good and evil, magic and mortality. I would have enjoyed exploring this character in a class even, not a production. I really enjoyed the learning aspect of it, more than anything else. The performing aspect of it was the frustrating part!

Q:. HOW DID YOU GO ABOUT GETTING THE ACCENT, THE POSTURE, YOUR WAY OF MOVING AROUND? HOW DID YOU WORK OUT THOSE PHYSICAL ELEMENTS?

A: Without a lot of thought, actually. Accents are something we've always played with in the house. You wake up some morning and everybody's got a Scottish brogue at breakfast. And you think nothing of it – it's just something we do in our house. We're a very loud family when we're home. I was like that. Tim [the director of *The Tempest*, Tim Evans] actually said it was supposed to be like a Caribbean-Indian accent. There was nothing online, nobody doing any kind of that accent like that that I saw. None of the Royal Shakespeare Company had anything close to that!

Q: I'VE TALKED TO A NUMBER OF ACTORS WHO HAVE DIFFERENT FEELINGS ABOUT WATCHING OTHER ACTORS PERFORM THEIR ROLES. DID YOU FIND IT AT ALL INTIMIDATING TO FIND SO MANY GREAT ACTORS TACKLING THIS PART? OR DID YOU FIND IT LIBERATING TO DISCOVER THERE WERE SO MANY WAYS TO DO THIS PART?

A: I would have been probably a lot more self-conscious, a lot more uptight, and things probably would have been different if I had been doing this for an established theatre company.

Q: BECAUSE?

A: Because people who know what they are doing would see it! [laughs]

Q: WOULD YOU HAVE LIKED A LITTLE MORE GUIDANCE, OR WERE YOU COMFORTABLE JUST FEELING YOUR WAY THROUGH THE ROLE?

A: I actually sought out a lot of help from anybody in the cast who had done any other show before. I cornered everybody, backstage and in-between rehearsals. Every line I think I ran by somebody who clearly knew a lot more than I did.

Q: SO MUCH HAS BEEN WRITTEN ABOUT *THE TEMPEST*. IT'S PROBABLY ONE OF THE MOST HEAVILY ANALYZED PLAYS—

A: That was helpful. I read a lot of that criticism, and there were videos of everything from the Royal Shakespeare Company to various companies around the U.S. who have done productions, as well as the recent film that came out with Helen Mirren and that probably helped me not only with my part, but to get my head around the entire storyline. That helped put what I was doing in the right context. I'm like, "Ok, there's this piece, and then there's this piece, and then my scene, and I see now how it all fits together." You see not just your part but the whole play. Anytime you're reading a part, I imagine you're knee-deep in that. You know, my kids come to me after a show and say, "How did that scene go? I've never seen it." And that's probably the biggest tragedy of any of the kids' work: they never get to see their own show. So for me, watching the movie helped with the larger context.

Q: DID YOUR CONCEPTION OF YOUR CHARACTER, OR THE MEANING OF THE PLAY, CHANGE IN THE COURSE OF SPENDING TIME WORKING ON THE ROLE? DID YOU COME TO DISCOVER SOME THINGS ABOUT CALIBAN THAT SURPRISED YOU? DID YOU COME TO LIKE HIM, OR DISLIKE HIM, MORE THAN YOU EXPECTED?

A: It's all to the positive. When Tim first described it, I really just thought it was some cartoon-ish character. If all you read is the first scene, that's what you come away with. But as I spent more time digging into the play, reading what had been written about him, the happier I was with this role. You start thinking, "This is really cool." It got to the point where it almost didn't matter if anybody was going to show up to watch it. Just being able to do this is really kind of cool.

Q: WATCHING YOU PERFORM THE ROLE, IT WAS AMONG THE MOST PHYSICAL OF CALIBANS I'VE SEEN...THE CRAWLING, THE JUMPING, THE RUNNING AROUND, THE COWERING. WHAT TO YOU

WAS MORE DIFFICULT — THE PHYSICAL ASPECTS OF PERFORMANCE, THROWING YOURSELF AROUND WITH SUCH FEROCITY, OR THE LANGUAGE, WHICH IS SO RICH?

A: It was always the language. The other part, the physical, you don't really think about it. Okay, throw another log on the fire. I knew if I did it differently every night, it wouldn't really matter. But I felt really compelled to try to get the language right. The memorization, the learning of the lines was something I never had to do before. My daughter actually helped me out the most, giving me neumonic help in terms of memorizing, chunking the text, tying it to emotion, tying it to reaction – just real acting skills. It was delightful working with my 15-year-old daughter, having her teach me how to do this. And I think she enjoyed being able to use something from her world to help her old man out. So that was a lot of fun at home.

Q: DID YOU FIND YOURSELF IN THE COURSE OF YOUR DAY THINKING ABOUT, EVEN PRACTICING, YOUR LINES? HOW MUCH OF THE ROLE LEECHED INTO YOUR LIFE?

A: It became inseparable. Just the time it takes to get the role down, it kind of became ridiculous.

Q: CALIBAN IS SO MUCH AN EXOTIC, BIZARRE, FORCEFUL CHARACTER, AND CAN BE PLAYED SO MANY WAYS, AS YOU NOTED. WHAT DID YOU WANT THE AUDIENCE TO THINK ABOUT YOUR CALIBAN — HOW SHOULD THEY FEEL ABOUT HIM?

A: Well, I should say this is not an original idea, but if there's anything I tried to do, it was to have people wind up pitying the character by the end of the play. That's kind of where I wound up. I wanted it to go from a kind of vile reaction, to understanding there's a whole lot more, to "Oh, what a shame!" If you think about it, he gets abandoned at the end of the play. So if anybody bothers to think about what happens when' the sun comes up the next day, he's stuck on the rock. And that's just the end of it. He's going to die alone on the island.

Q: SO IS THERE A MORAL TO *THE TEMPEST*?

A: I think for me, there's a definite forgiveness and a "second chance" theme that kind of runs through it. Everything from Ariel being released from the tree to the young lovers at the end being discovered, the play moves from worst-case to best-case. The fact that it starts out with three ships full of people drowning, and then, at the end it's "Oh no, everybody's fine. Don't worry – the ships didn't sink, they are ahead of you, but we're going to supply a strong wind, and you'll catch up. The King will return to rule, the Prince is alive, and we're all going back to Italy where the principalities will be restored." So it's all pretty good – except for the poor bastard that got stuck on the rock!

# Susan Nelle

> **❝** *When you start a new play, a new role, it's daunting. You're thinking 'I've got to find this character somewhere in me.' That process is challenging, frightening, stimulating, exhilarating.* **❞**

*Susan Nelle, who holds a Ph.D. from the University of Washington, recently re-ignited her interest in theatre and performance. A former management consultant, she is a graduate of a two-year training program at the Portland Actors Conservatory. Dividing her time between Australia and the United States, she has been seen in a variety of roles, from contemporary works to Shakespeare, and from stage to film. Highlights include the Duchess of York in Richard III, "A" in Three Tall Women, and Amanda in The Glass Menagerie.*

Q: Do you remember your first encounter with Shakespeare?

A: Well, not specifically what plays, but I do remember going to Ashland, when I lived in San Francisco, for the Oregon Shakespeare Festival. The whole Shakespeare experience there was wonderful.

In terms of performing, I got re-introduced to Shakespeare when I went to the Conservatory [Portland Actors Conservatory] That would be when I first encountered really working with the language.

Q: DID YOU STUDY SHAKESPEARE AT ALL IN HIGH SCHOOL?

A: In high school it didn't make much of an impression on me.

Q: SO WHAT GOT YOU INVOLVED IN THEATRE?

A: When I was growing up, I got introduced to the theatre because I was very shy, and my mother took me to creative drama classes when I was eight or nine to help me with my shyness. When I was ten or eleven, I studied at the Pittsburgh Playhouse and I auditioned for a show that played in schools – and I got it. It was a story about Norwegian children who carried gold bullion on their sleighs. When I was in high school, I was in *Our Town*. I was in *Matchmaker*, and the summer before I got married, I did Summer Stock in Pittsburgh, and went out to their local summer theatre. Basically, started off as an apprentice, and then got cast in the lead in a Tennessee Williams play, *Period of Adjustment*.

Then, I got married and moved to Arkansas, and didn't really do anything there. And then I did just a couple of other shows, but I was working as a management consultant and traveled a lot. When I first moved to Australia – where I lived for twenty-five years – I did a couple of things, but not really serious because I didn't have the time. I do remember auditioning for *All My Sons* in Australia, and I got a call back, and got right down to the last two, but I didn't get the part.

44

Q: Based on your years in Australia, would you say that there's a thriving Shakespeare scene there? Is it as intense as it is in, say, England?

A: English directors have said that the U.S. is kind of unique in its obsession with Shakespeare. There are festivals in the park everywhere in the summer in the U.S., and that's not true in England and Australia.

Q: Would you agree that Shakespeare has to be seen to be appreciated? And what led to your appreciation of his works?

A: When I took the Shakespeare class at the conservatory, I really began to appreciate the language, the power of the language. One of the first things you have to do if you want to honor the language is to break it down, really try to understand it. In the language, Shakespeare gives you the emotions. You don't have to manufacture the emotions, the language will tell you the state of mind that the speaker is in, as well as the facts of the story. It made me appreciate even more good writing – even good American writing. When I did Tennessee Williams' *Glass Menagerie*, it's very similar. I discovered a rhythm and feel in the language, which I learned by studying Shakespeare.

Q: And you've now moved from studying it to performing it.

A: I basically am retired. One of the reasons why I didn't go on further myself is I remember hearing that in order to be a full-time performer, or member of the creative arts, you can't imagine yourself doing anything else. For me, I have a life outside of that, with friends, and things I like to do. But it's now a chance for me to explore a road not taken. I love performing now because it's important to keep spirit and energy in your life.

It's been wonderful. The first show that I auditioned for while I was studying – a summer show – I didn't get cast. The first show I did was *King John* – I had a small role, but it was enough to get me involved with the theatre company [Northwest Classical Theatre Company]. Just yesterday, we closed with *Richard III* and that was terrific. The director was wonderful, and he kept telling us we needed to pick up the pace. First, you've got to unpack the language and figure out what it means, and then you have to put it all back together and then tell the story. It takes some time to figure out how to communicate the language and the story. You have to learn when to breathe. We were taking just a bit too long.

Q: WELL, MASTERING THE LANGUAGE IS A REAL CHALLENGE.

A: One of the things that Shakespeare teaches you is you really have to learn where to pause. Shakespeare has put in the pauses for you, and you need to take them when they come up. That's the thing about Shakespeare's language – you have to learn to trust it. It is everything, Everything will fit in and around it if you are true to the language.

Q: AND AUDIENCES WILL FOLLOW ALONG?

A: There are some directors that think an audience won't get it, and they feel like they have to add shtick to it, but I believed – and now I know – you don't have to. The language is all. You don't have to overdo it – the humor is there, no need to overdo it. Just trust the language.


Q: IT SOUNDS LIKE YOUR EXPERIENCE PERFORMING SHAKESPEARE HAS BEEN POSITIVE – EVEN A BIT OF A REVELATION.

A: Shakespeare is new and alive to me. I hope to continue. I'd like to do *Lear.* Sometime, I hope to be able to find a director who is willing to take a chance and cast me as *King Lear.* I'd like to try. Why not?


Q: *LEAR* IS A CHALLENGE TO SAY THE LEAST. JUST LEARNING ALL THOSE LINES WOULD BE GRUELING.

A: You know what I love? I didn't understand this until recently. I really love the rehearsal process – even more than performing. That's the creative process, that's where the learning comes in. Working on *Richard III*, we had a really great cast, great chemistry. That doesn't just happen. It takes *work*. You have to become familiar enough with the text, early enough, that you can really do the work. That's what you learn in drama school, that it's not about you, it's about the other actor or actors. Learning to play with those people, working out the things you need to tell the story, that's the hard work of rehearsal. In a good rehearsal process, you're exploring what makes it come alive, what moves it. If it's not alive, it's just someone standing up there reading from a textbook.

For instance, if your character is angry, you explore what's under the anger, what's driving it. In the performance it happens. In rehearsal, you're *making* it happen.

Q: WHY DO YOU THINK SOME PEOPLE COMMIT SO DEEPLY TO PERFORMANCE, EVEN WHEN THERE OFTEN IS LITTLE OR NO PROFIT IN IT?

A: I can't answer for everyone. I can answer for me. How you approach whatever you are doing can become a creative process. When you start a new play, a new role, it's daunting. You're thinking "I've got to find this character *somewhere* in me." That process is challenging, frightening, stimulating, exhilarating. I think the chance to create that kind of art together, when it really works, it's magic. There's a bit of magic there. And then you want to come back to it. It isn't the being on the stage that's important to me. It's my participating in telling a story that I think is important to tell.

It's the opportunity to create something that's meaningful for yourself but also, when it works, touches the lives of people who come to see it. Theatre does it in a way that is truly different from film. There's nothing like the intimacy of being in a small theater, because the audience is a part of the play. When it works, it's so memorable, so exciting.

Q: DO YOU WATCH FILMS TO SEE HOW OTHERS HAVE PERFORMED CERTAIN ROLES?

A: I happened to be watching TV and I saw Ian McKellen doing *Richard*. We did it totally different, but his performance was impressive. Other than that, I haven't sought out Shakespeare films.

Q: HOW DO YOU FEEL ABOUT DIRECTORS BEING INNOVATIVE, CHANGING THE SETTING OR THE TIME FRAME IN WHICH THE PLAYS ARE SET?

A: I think that's fine, so long as you honor the language. We did that with our *Richard*. The director wanted this to be an American production, so we used video imagery, and he wanted to remind Americans that we had our own civil war, and that there are elements tearing at this country right now. He pointed out that Shakespeare wrote in two time frames: for the audience of his contemporaries, but also about events from history. The issues of power struggles happen now, they are today's issues, so we were in modern dress. If the director really knows the play, and knows what he or she is trying to say, then I think it can be made even more powerful and accessible. You don't have to prance around in medieval outfits. The plays are about timeless themes and struggles – but you have to honor the language of the story.

Q: WHAT'S NEXT FOR YOU, AS A PERFORMER?

A: I will always try to keep working to find opportunities to be in good Shakespeare productions. If you can do that honestly, handle the language, and make the character real, then you know that you can do almost anything. To me, that's the gold standard.

# Tel Monks

> **" Someone who is serious about what we're doing – it's play, but it's also serious – and wants to have contact, really communicate to the audience, is someone I enjoy working with and respect."**

*Born in the London area, Tel Monks attended a public (i.e. restricted entrance) all-boys school in Wandsworth and started acting at the age of 14, at first playing female roles until his voice broke. At this school much of the time in English class was spent reading Shakespeare, and his first introduction was by way of Julius Caesar. From there he went to Exeter University to study modern languages. Since there was no Drama Department there at the time, students formed their own Dramatic Society.*

*Since moving to the United States, Tel became active in Community Theatre and played the part of Macbeth, and later, Polonius in Hamlet. When he started acting professionally, in classical and experimental theatre, the only Shakespeare role (so far) was Antonio in Much Ado about Nothing at the Folger Shakespeare Theatre in Washington DC. He is still active in the Washington Area, although his only claim to 'fame' has been as Father Lewandowski in the TV series "The Wire."*

51

Q: WHEN DID YOU FIRST ENCOUNTER SHAKESPEARE?

A: Our equivalent of high school includes middle school. That was my first experience with his text. Around that time, we had seen Laurence Olivier doing his film of *Hamlet*. From the secondary class, we did Shakespeare regularly. Also Dickens. Dickens we would read, going around the class. Shakespeare we would stand up, and perform it. But there was very little thought given to *how* to perform it. There's not too much behind your performance when your 11 years old. But it did reinforce the idea that Shakespeare was to be performed.

Q: WAS THERE A DRAMA CLUB AT YOUR SCHOOL?

A: There was indeed. – that's how I got started in acting. Until I was about 14, I had a very pronounced stammer. I was very nervous about public speaking, reading from a play, reading around the class was a dreadful experience. When I was 14 an English teacher obliged me to read for a part in the play. He cast me as Cecily in the *Importance of Being Earnest*. From that time, I pretty much got rid of my stammer. My teacher, who was absolutely brilliant but was remarkably strict, and could reduce me to tears, helped me master how to deliver the lines.

Then I was fortunate enough to go to a university [Exeter] that had no drama department – which meant we could all be in the plays. You still had to audition, but if they liked you, you were in. In three years, I must have done eight different plays. We even took some of these plays on tour, and I was in *Taming of the Shrew*. That was my first really serious experience.

I had been doing some extra work in the movies during vacations, then when I left Exeter and went to graduate school in

London, my roommate was the John Gielgud scholar there. And *he* never got an acting job, which was very disillusioning. I was in a technical area there, kind of early computer science. I decided acting was a gamble that wasn't likely to pay off for me.

Q: WHEN DID YOU MOVE TO THE UNITED STATES – AND WHY?

A: I moved here in 1967. I came here for a job – an American company that had come over to head hunt, they picked up half a dozen people, and I worked for them for a couple of years. I was in computational linguistics. I was working very hard, and I didn't get back into acting for some time. After my son was born, we moved to Reston, Va., and I saw they were doing a play there. They had a theatre group, and they were doing a comedy. So I did it, and it was a successful experience. I stayed with the Reston players for years. They did a Shakespeare play – *Macbeth*. I played a Scotsman. Once we were here in Reston, that was about 1973, there was really not much here. It was like a dormitory town – very different from what is here today. There's the question of what do you do when you're out here. So I joined the Reston Community Players, both as an actor and director.

Q: WHY DIRECTING?

A: I always wanted to. When I was in Exeter, and we took *Taming of the Shrew* on the road. I was the assistant director. And then the director couldn't go on the road, so I became the director. When I came back, I still wanted to do it. Almost any show you're in, one could see gaps, and I'd think, "I could do that differently."

Q: YOU'VE HAD A GREAT DEAL OF EXPERIENCE WITH
SHAKESPEARE. DO YOU EVER THINK ABOUT THE IMPACT HIS WORKS
HAVE HAD ON YOU?

A: How did Shakespeare change my life? It was always there, since I was 10 or 11. He was always present. We did *Julius Caesar* in class, *The Tempest, The Winter's Tale.* For the equivalent of your high school graduation exams, we did *Hamlet,* and really had to pick the play apart. Shakespeare was always large in my life.

Q: HAS THAT MADE IT EASIER TO PERFORM SHAKESPEARE,
HAVING A HISTORY WITH THE WORKS?

A: I think Shakespeare is always daunting. Just the idea that you are putting something across to an audience that is not in a vernacular they are familiar with, that's a real challenge. The idea of putting on a good *King Lear* is almost impossible. I played Macbeth – I did not do a good job of it. It's too tough. I did not like it myself, but I did what I was asked to do by the director.

Q: DO YOU THINK AMERICAN ACTORS ARE MORE INTIMIDATED,
OR LESS COMFORTABLE, WITH SHAKESPEARE THAN BRITISH ACTORS?

A: Having done Shakespeare plays for American audiences, I didn't notice any special reticence, or fear being shown, among the Americans.

Q: HOW DO YOU PREPARE FOR A ROLE?

A: I just did a role in community theatre. I was in *Equus.* I was the psychiatrist, Dysart. When I heard it was going to be cast, I started reading up. I got the play, and some months in advance I started working on the monologues, so that I understood every word the author had written. I guess my technique is to elevate the text. To me the text is paramount. You want to work with the text and create as seamless a performance as possible so that that text is the only possible thing that character could say. I don't think many playwrights would disagree with that. Edward Albee is like that. The Albee Association will attend plays, with the text in their laps, following every word. They want to make sure you are saying the play exactly. There was a production of *Who's Afraid of Virginia Woolf?* that they actually shut down because they veered from the text.

Q: Does that text-based interpretation ever conflict with a director's vision? And do you prefer a more activist, or a more passive director?

A: An activist director is fine. If I find someone who disagrees with me, I will try in good faith to do what they want for their show. I wil try to communicate their vision, as well as my own, of course. When I played Macbeth, I was not in agreement always with the director's vision. When I was in *Hamlet*, I played Polonious. I had my own view of Polonius, and the director left me alone to go with it in the direction I wanted. The last show I did, *Equus,* my director was extremely supportive. She was very open, but she would still step in and adjust what I was doing, which I was very happy to have adjusted. The director who just says "Go and do it your way" is not really very much help.

Q: What do you learn from your fellow actors when you're on stage?

A: I study them. I do pay attention to them – I get the feeling that we're in this together. Someone who is serious about what we're doing – it's play, but it's also serious – and wants to have contact, really communicate to the audience, is someone I enjoy working with and respect. There are people who come in in a kind of a vacuum but don't make contact with other people on stage – do the role, collect their money, go home. Sometimes contact is unpleasant, but it's got to be there. There are some actors who come in and give you a flashy entrance, flashy exit, and that's it. But if they haven't made contact, it just doesn't work.

Q: ARE THERE ANY ROLES YOU'VE NEVER PERFORMED BUT WOULD LIKE TO?

A: Of course, I'm getting on a bit, but I'd love to play in *Whose Afraid of Virgina Woolf?*, *Amadeus* – I'd love to play Salieri. I've done comedy, and I love to do comedy, but the roles that I'd most like to do are dramas. I'd love to take a shot at Prospero in *The Tempest*. I'm not sure I could handle it – but I'd like to try.

# Nate Paine

*" One night, it was raining pretty good...but we still went on, and about 50 people sat in the rain and watched the play. We must have been pretty good for them to sit there in the rain.* "

Born in Washington, Nate Paine grew up among the wheat fields and apple orchards of Eastern Oregon. Most of his time was spent bickering with his younger brother, as two older brothers left just a few years after his birth. He dabbled in the performing arts through school plays and church pageants, but most of his time was spent reading fantasy and science fiction novels.

Nate really began his amateur acting career in college at Northwest Nazarene University. He was cast as Lysander in Shakespeare's A Midsummer Night's Dream. Since then, he has been played such parts as Commander Harbison in South Pacific, Horatio in Hamlet, and Caliban in The Tempest.

Nate currently lives in Idaho with his two cats Spade and Finnick.

Q: WHAT WAS YOUR FIRST ENCOUNTER WITH SHAKESPEARE?

A: The first time I remember encountering Shakespeare was in high school, junior year English class. *Macbeth*. And I'm sure I encountered it before then. My mom was an English major, and she really enjoys Shakespeare. We acted it out a bit in class, in an abridged version. We had a little group, and we'd take one scene and then three or four of us would do that scene, just for the class.

Q: HOW'D YOU LIKE THAT?

A: I liked the story of *Macbeth*. It didn't necessarily make me want to pursue Shakespeare more, but I did enjoy it.

Q: ANY OTHER MEMORIES OF SHAKESPEARE IN HIGH SCHOOL?

A: I remember seeing a PBS special, the "Abridged Shakespeare Company," and they did all these silly abridged Shakespeare performances. It was really hilarious. That really got me hooked, and probably did more to get me interested in Shakespeare. My parents – they didn't really enjoy the regular content that was on tv – sitcoms, dramas…but they did enjoy what PBS put out, so we would watch those shows as a family.

The next time I came across Shakespeare wasn't in a classroom but on stage. It was my junior year of college, and the people I became friends with were kind of theatre nerds, but I was a little stage shy, so I never got on stage until my junior year, until someone convinced me that they needed guys to try out. So I tried out. I talked to the director and said "I've never really acted before, and what I have done is Christmas programs at church, and I'm not really comfortable, so if I could get a minor part...." He said "No problem," and when the cast list came out, I got the part of Lysander!

Q: WHAT WAS YOUR REACTION?

A: At first, I was overwhelmed. This is a little bigger than I expected. Being the first real stage production I was in, it took me a while to get used to the idea of acting on stage.

It wasn't difficult for me to memorize. It was more difficult to understand what I was saying. That's what my director was stressing, making sure the audience understood what we were saying. He wasn't as interested in worrying about reciting the meter as it was written, with all the stresses, but to speak it with normal inflection. It was also difficult for me to be larger than life on stage....it's one of Shakespeare's comedies, and the characters are not what you'd call `normal.' They're blown out of proportion. That was a little difficult for me. It was also difficult since Lysander is one of the lovers, and it was difficult to have the character get romantically engaged. But it was also really fun. I really enjoyed it. Because of that experience, I've continued to perform.

Q: SO THAT WAS A SORT OF TRANSFORMING EXPERIENCE?

A: Definitely. Getting toward the end of rehearsals, I was beginning to see how awesome it is to create a show on stage. That really got me thinking about what else I might enjoy. That semester was also the semester that I switched to being a mass communication major. It kind of gave me more of an idea of a direction to go in life. I still don't necessarily know where I'm going, but I have a direction in which I'm going to push. It also gave me Shakespeare, who for a lot of people is really difficult to understand, but once I understood him, and I got the jokes, I began reading more Shakespeare, and have gotten into his works, trying to study them more closely.

Every semester, we have a stage play in the fall and then we have a musical in the spring. And after Shakespeare, I tried out for the musical. *Fiddler on the Roof,* and got to play a part in that. I was the Constable. Then I did the show in the fall, which was two one-act plays. The one I was in was *The Complete History of the Old Testament in 20 Minutes,* and then I was in the musical in the spring play the next year, *The Music Man.*

After *Fiddler on the Roof,* the musical director convinced me to join the general choir.

Q: WHAT HAPPENED AFTER YOU GRADUATED? DID YOU STILL PERFORM?

A: After I was done with school in 2008, I was focusing on work and trying to figure out what I wanted to do, so it took me a couple of years after school to get back on stage. The first thing I did was a kid's musical about the legend of Pecos Bill. The troupe is called Encore Theatre, here in Nampa. Jonathan Perry, the director I had worked with at school, he and his wife and a few other people started the troupe. They called me up: "Hey, we really need some more guys to try out." I was eager to get back on stage. It was fun – I got to act with a lot of people I never met before. We got close. There were a couple of people who were in school at NNU, and over time, we've become pretty good friends.

Q: Have you performed Shakespeare since graduating?

A: Summer 2012, Encore did a production of *Hamlet*, and I played Horatio. Well, *Hamlet* is one of my favorite Shakespeare plays. I was really excited to be a part of that. I did try out for the part of Hamlet, but I got Horatio, which was my second choice. We performed in a little outdoor amphitheater, and that was my first time to perform in a setting like that. We had 30 to 50 people a night, and it was a lot of fun. I felt good about the play. Being outside you're exposed to the elements. One night, it was raining pretty good, and the power went out in the building next to us, but we still went on, and about 50 people sat in the rain and watched the play. We must have been pretty good for them to sit there in the rain.

Q: As a young actor, did the idea of performing *Hamlet*, which is such a landmark play, intimidate you at all?

A: It's kind of daunting to think about the history that you are a part of when you're doing Shakespeare, especially one of the big plays like *Hamlet*. You just have to sit back and say to yourself: *I'm going out there.* The people most likely know the story because it's been done, not only on stage but in movies and in lots of different forms. Just being able to give that to people is a real pleasure.

Q: Are there any other Shakespeare roles you'd like to perform?

A: I'd really like to take a part in *Richard II*. I'm not old enough to play *Richard II*, but to be in that play would be fun. I really enjoy the tragedies. *Richard II* is a history play, but it's really a tragic story. *Othello* would be another production I'd love to be a part of.

Q: WHAT HAVE YOU GAINED FROM YOUR FELLOW ACTORS?

A: Just being able to observe them, both while I'm on stage with them and when I'm offstage, watching, trying to get the feel for how big they are on stage. I still struggle with being larger than life so that the people in the back of the theater can see what I'm trying to emote on stage. That's really what I've learned. Also, situational awareness…if the blocking doesn't go right, how others cope with that.

The biggest thing I've learned from performing Shakespeare is getting an understanding of what you're saying. The language he was writing in is so far removed from the language we use today. It's not so much the words you are speaking, it's how you are saying it, your actions, your body language. That's what can make or kill a Shakespeare production, in my opinion – creating an understanding, an understanding for the audience so they can know what's happening.

Q: SO DO YOU PAY ATTENTION TO HOW ACTORS DO THAT, EVEN IN NON-SHAKESPEARE PERFORMANCES?

A: Yeah, I think that would be true for me, even watching tv or movies. When I'm looking at someone as an actor, I will watch a number of their films together, to see how they put together a character. I look at what kind of business they do, how they will use inflection to help create the character in dialect. I really enjoy Alec Baldwin as Jack Donaghy in *30 Rock* – his character is so masculine. He tries so hard and he's very successful at being a man's man, but he is still able to have touching emotional moments with people he cares about. In his strength you can still see his vulnerability.

Q: LIKE HAMLET?

A: Yes – especially in those moments when he's struggling with the idea of going insane, and in those scenes with Horatio and his mother. You *see* his vulnerability.

# Jon Ciccarelli

**" The more you perform Shakespeare, the more your realize it was written by an actor who worked in the same circumstances that you're toiling in yourself. "**

*Jon Ciccarelli is originally from Ischia, Italy and grew up in Madison, NJ. Jon was bitten by the acting bug early and performed his first full length play in sixth grade and appeared in various acting class showcases and full length plays throughout his time at Madison High School and Seton Hall University. A love of Shakespeare did not come easy for this future artistic director. After constantly being told he had to try it in order to really test his acting chops, he got into productions of "Alls Well That Ends Well" as one of the Dumain brothers and Antonio in "The Tempest" and he found -"hmmm, there's something to this".*

*In 1996, a chance recommendation by a fellow actor led Jon to audition for an eccentric Jersey City, NJ native named L. Robert "Luther" Johnson for a production of "Hamlet" where he landed the role of Horatio. The pair struck up a long and fruitful friendship where they joined forces and produced over 100 Shakespeare and modern touring shows until Luther's untimely death in 2010. Jon carries on his legacy by continuing Hudson Shakespeare Company's primary mission of out of the box Shakespeare titles and concepts. Some of Jon's notable Shakespeare and classical roles include Hamlet, Macbeth, Falstaff, Iago, and Richard III His notable Shakespeare directing credits include Cardenio, Henry VIII, Timon of Athens, Pericles, Cymbeline, Henry V, all-female Julius Caesar, Much Ado About Nothing, Macbeth and Hamlet.*

*In his off time from theatrical endeavors he works as Quality Assurance analyst and Technical Writer in testing and documenting websites, mobile apps and other software packages. He is married to his fellow Shakespeare partner in crime Noelle Fair, who he met in a Hudson Shakespeare show.*

Q: WHERE DID YOU GROW UP, WHERE DID YOU GO TO SCHOOL — AND HOW IS IT YOU ENDED UP AT THE HELM OF THE HUDSON SHAKESPEARE COMPANY?

A: Basically, I'm New Jersey raised. I grew up in Madison, New Jersey. Originally from Italy, my family came here when I was three years old. I've always had the acting bug. Had it from like when I was seven years old. Did the usual kind of school plays. And trained…actually, I was fortunate enough to have a theatre program in high school, so I did that all four years. For college, I went to Seton Hall.

Q: WERE YOUR PARENTS ARTISTIC?

A: Not at all.

Q: TO WHAT DO YOU ATTRIBUTE YOUR EARLY APTITUDE FOR THE ARTS?

A: Honestly, it seems like the thing I was naturally drawn to. My very first thing was a Christmas pageant. I did that at a local lodge. They needed kids to be the shepherds, and whatever. They actually had live animals, you know, as opposed to people playing sheep. So that was kind of like my first foray into the theatre. It was the excitement, the adrenaline rush of doing that. In sixth grade, I had my first lead in a play called *The King's Cream Puffs*. There were like thirty-five pages of dialogue. My sixth grade teacher wanted to produce a play. Every guy in class was pretty much afraid of taking on the King's part because it required so much memorization. So by the time I got the part, it was two weeks before we had to go up. So I did a crash course in trying to memorize thirty-five pages of dialogue, where other characters had very short scenes, two, three pages.

Q: Do you remember feeling anxious about that?

A: Oh, I was both elated and nervous as anything. I remember distinctly the process where I would just try to learn by rote, you know, just repeat it repeat it repeat it, and that worked out fairly well. The day of the performance – there was only one performance – as soon as the curtains parted, it started out with me sleeping on a throne, waking up, and then figuring out what the king was going to do that day. And he has this, you know, insatiable love of cream puffs [laughs]. So I remember, curtain parted, I opened my eyes and there's like about eight hundred students with parents and whatnot all looking at me, and I was like `Oh my freaking God!' But then you just go into what you had done in rehearsal and it flowed. I had butterflies, but you just get to a point where it's like on auto pilot, and then from there my next few plays in high school were a lot of the same thing. I auditioned for pieces, I did mostly class work. The things I did in high school were mostly classic, twentieth century, where it was, you know, Neil Simon, and Arthur Miller.

Q: Can you give me a sense of how active an arts community your high school had?

A: It was actually a very big commitment to arts. We had a large classroom, like two classrooms in one, with a purpose-built stage. The teacher that I had, his name was Joe Russo. I still credit him – you know, one of those people that actors refer back to as those who shaped their outlook and whatnot. He was a major influence, and he insisted that everyone call him by his first name, which was pretty anathema at the time, but he was like, "No, call me Joe." He was like an ex-flower child. He would insist on calling everyone Brother Love and Sister Love. He didn't necessarily dress the part, but he still maintained that kind of free-thinking kind of thing. The first part of the year was basically interacting. We talked about what blocking meant, what was upstage, downstage, how to face out, what was the fourth wall, that kind of thing, and then the second half was theatre in repertory. The first thing I ever did there was from *The Crucible*. And it was interesting because I've ended up doing *The Crucible* through the years like five times, in various parts,.

Q: Do you remember your first encounter with Shakespeare?

A: I was failing freshman English. Which was kind of strange because English had always been one of my better subjects. We were doing *Romeo and Juliet* and *The Merchant of Venice* that year, and I could not get into it to save my life. I was reading it, I was thinking, "Oh, this is a play, I'm really into this stuff, this should be a breeze." But I just didn't understand the wording, I had some exposure to *Romeo and Juliet* from the movie…your typical teenage exposure to the play. But aside from that I hated the subject. My first thing was, my teacher was offering extra credit where if

70

you memorized a speech from the *Merchant of Venice*, which was Portia's "The quality of mercy is not strained," she would give you the equivalent of a test grade, like an A. And I needed it. So I was like, "This is fantastic. I'll memorize this, I'm an actor, this will be the easiest A I've ever gotten." So then, I had the worst time trying to memorize that. Again, nothing made sense. I actually despised it. So the day came, and I had about two thirds memorized. So I was waiting there for the teacher. She had a meeting that day, so she was late. There I am, sitting there, after school, wanting just to get the hell out of there, and half an hour went by, and she didn't come by yet, and I remember thinking to myself, "This asshole has been dead five hundred years and he's screwing up my life now!"

Q: SO DID YOU EVER GET A CHANCE TO RECITE THE SPEECH?

A: Yes I did. She finally showed up, said the meeting that she was in ran late. So I did it, but I basically, again, screwed up about maybe about a third of the speech. But she was like, "Okay, that's fine." But it was like the most unconnected thing I had ever done. So basically, at that point, I was resigned to the fact that this is not for me. I don't care what anybody says, I don't want to do it. And whenever this came up in acting class, I was like "I don't want to do Shakespeare." You know – *anything* but that. But then, as I got into college, I always picked actors' brains about what monologues they were doing, and it would always come back to "Well, I'm memorizing a Shakespeare monologue," and I'm like "Why? It's so dull, blah blah blah." And then one actor told me that if you really want to get better, if you really want to test your mettle, you really should do this, because if you can do this then you're not just a fly-by-night intern. It means you actually have what it takes. And in my acting, I had always been told that I had natural ability. I'm like, "All right, if I'm actually thinking that I'm good at this, then let me try this and see what happens."

An opportunity to perform it in college never really came up, so out of college I auditioned for a production of *The Tempest*. And I got the role of Antonio – which was the villain. And it was with a director who had worked both Off-Broadway and Off-Off Broadway. So this director really took an interest how I approached the speeches. He was looking for someone who could really bring life to this villain. It's kind of a cardboard cutout villain. So we rehearsed quite a bit in those specific scenes, and it was a really interesting learning period, just working off of his feedback. And unfortunately, the person who was organizing it, really had his head up his ass. He lost the venue – we didn't have a place to rehearse. We were losing people. At that point, I had some local connections, so I told the theatre director, "Hey listen, I can get you some people and I can get you a place to rehearse." I didn't realize at the time but what I was doing then, contacting people, getting them together to rehearse and scheduling places, was exactly what I do now as Artistic Director. I was doing producing duties without even realizing it. Well, the production finally fell through, and I was very crestfallen at coming that close. What I desperately desired was to get into parts where I could really work, and hone my acting skills. I had gotten a taste of Antonio and the dialogue and the relationships and that thing that I had when I was 14, that hate, just evaporated.

Q: HOW LONG WAS IT BEFORE YOU WERE ABLE TO ACTUALLY PERFORM SHAKESPEARE?

A: Well, a couple of years later, my girlfriend at the time, said "Hey, I know you've been looking around for some Shakespeare opportunities," – they didn't really come up too often in community theatre. So she a saw a notice in the *Star-Ledger* for a company called Hudson Shakespeare Company, in Jersey City, and they were doing *Hamlet*. And I thought, "Okay, *Hamlet*, whoa. That's the big time." I had had a brush with Jersey City where I got cast in a bit part in something, and I was like, "The commute sucks...but what the hell, let me give it a shot."

Q: WHAT WAS THE COMPANY LIKE?

A: Being so close to New York, it was a mix of people who had worked together previously, and then New York-based actors who were trying to make it. They weren't in the union yet, but that's what they were trying to shoot for. Or they were working on TV, or in film, and that's still the same population the company has now.

Q: YOU WERE AN ACTOR WHO EVENTUALLY BECAME A DIRECTOR AS WELL. WHEN YOU WERE ACTING, WHAT WAS YOUR IMPRESSION OF THE DIRECTION YOU WERE GETTING -- WAS IT USEFUL? WERE YOU ALREADY SORT OF DIRECTING YOURSELF? WE'RE YOU A DIRECTOR'S ACTOR, OR DID YOU HAVE STRONG IDEAS ABOUT WHAT YOU SHOULD BE DOING?

A: I worked with directors, even some directors who I thoroughly enjoyed as an artist, and as a person, who would give me direction and I'm thinking to myself `You gotta be kidding me!" But I found I actually thrive in those situations, where you don't come out and just say "Hey, I think your direction is full of shit." I've worked with actors who go down that road, and very soon after they're not working any more.

Q: YOU WORK IN THE I.T. FIELD. BUT DID YOU EVER THINK ABOUT JUST GOING ALL OUT AND TRYING TO MAKE A FULL-TIME CAREER OUT OF ACTING AND DIRECTING?

A: I did initially before I joined Hudson Shakespeare. I did a few auditions locally, tried going into New York, but I never liked it. I could never see myself living there, you know sharing an apartment with four other strangers, and I knew that that type of auditioning was not for me. And trying to make a living at the same time, basically I decided to keep the day job and stay active doing community theatre. And that was rewarding and frustrating at the same time. I would commute all over the place, and you were subject to whatever shows they were doing. And I had a major desire to do more Shakespeare. I had gotten a taste of it.

Q: DID YOU FIND SHAKESPEARE MORE DIFFICULT THAN WHAT YOU HAD BEEN PERFORMING? AND DO YOU PREPARE DIFFERENTLY FOR SHAKESPEARE THAN YOU WOULD FOR A TENNESSEE WILLIAMS PLAY, OR A BECKETT PLAY?

A: In preparation, no. Same deal: lots of memorization, same effort to understand what the scene is about, what are you trying to get out of it. I would often read up on characters in play critiques for Shakespeare, and I found that the scholarly perspective actually informed my acting, or my directing. I sought out what scholars had to say about *Hamlet*, or some other play. I would pick up one of the Arden paperbacks, and I got more into what the intro would say than the play itself.

Q: HOW ABOUT WATCHING OTHER PRODUCTIONS OF SHAKESPEARE PLAYS — DID YOU SEEK OUT ANY WELL-REGARDED OR FAMOUS INTERPRETATIONS, SUCH AS OLIVIER'S *HAMLET*, OR

A: No, I like to watch what other people have done. I'm a real fan, and student, of Kenneth Branagh. He was one that I always admired because, though he was making a very good living with the RSC, he decided to strike out on his own, and he got funding and that's how *Henry V* came about. So I felt like he was a kindred spirit, in the sense that you have a nice sideline doing what you're doing – and in my case, that was community theatre – but I wanted more. I wanted to do projects that I could spearhead, and get people together who I could work with.

Q: And focus on Shakespeare.

A: The great thing about doing Shakespeare, as opposed to say, Arthur Miller, is that Shakespeare was an actor himself. There's a lot of sensibility that an actor has about how to do a scene that's in the language itself. There's a great quote from Adrian Noble, who was the head of the RSC for a long time, that there's direction in the lines themselves – the idea being that the more you read Shakespeare, the more you have a kinship through that, and also a kinship to that legacy. With actors, you do a show, then you leave. There's no record of it sometimes. If you tried looking up something from ten years ago, good luck. But I feel like actors themselves are kind of inheritors of Shakespeare himself, and the people he worked with. He wasn't just the God of English letters. He rubbed shoulders with his leading man, and all the other actors of his companies. He knew he could count on these players to do what he was asking. There's a real question about what is Shakespeare's, and what lines came from rehearsals as they worked. Maybe somebody improvised something that got put into the show, or you have the input of other writers....a lot of people don't realize that Shakespeare collaborated with other writers. So what was that process like? The more you perform Shakespeare, the more your realize it was written by an actor who worked in the same circumstances that you're toiling in yourself.

# Theresa Lyons

**" *Sure, I think women can play the male roles in Shakespeare. Helen Mirren played Prospero as Prospera. And I have heard that an all-female troupe performed Hamlet. It's not impossible.* "**

*Theresa Lyons has been involved in theatre (acting or studying) for twenty years. She has a two-year certificate in acting from New Theatre, Boston, a B.M. in Music from Berklee and a M.A. in Speech-language pathology from Montclair State. A full-time school SLP, she studied acting for summers at such places as Circle in the Square Theatre School and the NJ Shakespeare Festival. Favorite past NJ community theatre roles: The Mousetrap (Mollie/ Casewell), Skin of Our Teeth (Mrs. Antrobus), Crimes of the Heart (Lenny), and A Flea in Her Ear (Raymonde).*

*[Editor's Note: Theresa played Ariel in the same Montclair, New Jersey production of The Tempest in which the interviewer played Gonzalo – an experience she revisits later in the interview.]*

*Theresa grew up with a severely autistic nephew, mentally ill sister and sickly father. Music and acting were her expressive outlets. Currently single, Theresa lives in northern NJ with her mom, sister, three cats, one dog and a bearded dragon.*

Q: DO YOU REMEMBER YOUR FIRST ENCOUNTER WITH
SHAKESPEARE?

A: I do remember probably like, when I was 10 or so, going on
a field trip, and I don't recall where it was exactly, but I remember
seeing *Hamlet*, and it was this really big auditorium, and I just remember this actor just speaking out, and it was incredible. It was
like he was speaking directly to me. He was in the middle of this
auditorium, but he just had such a command, a presence that it
was something else. Quite overwhelming. I was kind of scared, actually, just being this 10 year old.

Q: AND *HAMLET* IS A PRETTY HEAVY PLAY TO DIGEST AT ANY AGE,
LET ALONE WHEN YOU'RE TEN.

A: Well I think I was about 10, I can't recall exactly. I was pretty
young.

Q: WAS THAT A SCHOOL FIELD TRIP?

A: Yes.

Q: MOVING FORWARD FROM THERE, DO YOU REMEMBER EVER
HAVING TO SIT IN A SCHOOL CLASSROOM AND HAVING TO READ
ALOUD FROM, SAY, *ROMEO AND JULIET*? OR ANY OTHER BRUSHES YOU
MIGHT HAVE HAD WITH SHAKESPEARE, IN OR OUT OF SCHOOL?

A: When I was a teenager? No, I can't really remember too
much about Shakespeare then. I remember more reading
*Antigone*– that really struck me. It wasn't until later on that I encountered Shakespeare. But I knew who he was – I just didn't get into his

works until I took the acting program [in Boston]. They had one semester that dealt with Shakespeare. They had a teacher there, I think she was with Shakespeare and Company in Massachusetts, and she came in and she helped us with monologues – we each got to read any monologue, and then she picked out monologues for each of us to perform. The one she gave me was from *As You Like It*. Phoebe. It was quite interesting. She's a shepherdess, you know, and she falls in love with Rosalind, who is disguised as a man. It was a really interesting monologue. I liked it, and it was fun.

Q: WAS IT ANXIETY-INDUCING AT ALL, TRYING TO MEMORIZE THOSE LINES?

A: A little bit, you know. There's that language, that heightened language, but she made it fun. And she gave us time to memorize it.

Q: NOW ARIEL WAS NOT YOUR FIRST STAB AT SHAKESPEARE. DO YOU REMEMBER THE FIRST TIME YOU MIGHT HAVE PERFORMED SHAKESPEARE OUTSIDE THE CLASSROOM? DO YOU REMEMBER YOUR FIRST SHAKESPEAREAN ROLE?

A: Let's see…the first Shakespearean thing that I did was actually a sonnet. Out teacher in that program [in Boston] had us choose a sonnet so that we could get our feet wet. That was good. She wanted us to get used to iambic pentameter. She had us analyze it and said if there's words you don't know, look them up.

Q: DO YOU REMEMBER THE SONNET?

A: I don't remember the number, but it starts off "They that have the power to hurt…" [recites next eight lines from memory] I don't remember how it goes after that. That was along time ago.

Q: DID THIS CLASS FOCUS MORE ON THE MEANING OF SHAKESPEARE, LOOKING AT THE TEXT, AND DOING ANALYSIS – OR WAS IT MORE PERFORMANCE BASED?

A: My voice teacher tried to work on approaching vowels from the body, where you *feel* the vowels, so she was focused on that. Other teachers were more performance based. You know, what the character is after. They did let us choose other monologues. I think I chose Desdemona. At the time, I was going through a bad relationship, and I could, you know, feel her pain [laughs].

Q: SO THIS SHAKESPEARE CLASS YOU HAD – DID YOU ENJOY IT?

A: Oh yes, I enjoyed it. But it kind of stopped there because we went on to more modern theatre. It was more of an introduction. Later on, I took a course at the Shakespeare Theatre of New Jersey. They had programs in the summer – eleven weeks for beginners, mostly college students.

Q: SO YOU MUST HAVE BEEN SOMEWHAT SERIOUS ABOUT MASTERING SHAKESPEARE. THAT'S A PRETTY HIGH-LEVEL ORGANIZATION. THEY HAVE AN EXCELLENT REPUTATION.

A: Yes, definitely. They do – and they get the directors involved in the course. You have a voice teacher, you take different classes, it's very intense. They also have you work behind the scenes. I worked in the costume shop. So when they have a professional production going on, they had us do things here and there.

They did *Hamlet* that summer, and Lilly Taylor did Ophelia. They get actors from all over the country and Canada. The quality was great. We got to see a couple productions – it was inspiring. And it showed me how much work it takes to be a professional.


Q: Did you ever think about trying to make it as an actress full time, maybe go to New York, try to get an agent, go on auditions?

A: Well, I'm not sure how to do all that, but I did go to New York to study. In 2002, I went to Circle in the Square, and I did a seven-week program. That was something else – I *loved* Circle in the Square. They have such a great, great program. And I learned so much within seven weeks. That really opened my eyes to modern theatre. And you know what, if the stars had aligned and I could have done anything I wanted to do, I would have just kept doing that. But I took it for what it was.


Q: Have you performed one role in Shakespeare that you've loved more than any other? And do you have a dream role you'd like to perform?

A: Well, when I was in my 20s, I wanted to be a female Hamlet. And I still do! I would love to tackle Hamlet. That's one of the best roles Shakespeare ever wrote.


Q: And women have played that role—

A: Sure, I think women can play the male roles in Shakespeare. Helen Mirren played Prospero as Prospera. And I have heard that an all-female troupe performed *Hamlet*. It's not impossible. So if

I could pick and choose, it would be that. I always wanted to play Juliet – of course, I'm now too old to play her, but I love her monologues, they're just so beautiful. And the range of emotion she has.

Q: LET'S TALK A LITTLE BIT ABOUT *THE TEMPEST*, AND ARIEL. THAT'S A CHALLENGING ROLE – THERE'S A LOT OF COLORS ON THAT PALETTE. IT'S BEEN PERFORMED LOTS OF DIFFERENT WAYS ON STAGE, AND IN FILM. AND A LOT HAS BEEN WRITTEN ABOUT ARIEL. IN PREPARING FOR THAT ROLE, WHAT INSIGHTS DID YOU HAVE INTO ARIEL'S CHARACTER?

A: It was the duality – it could be a he or a she. When I started to research different productions, I mainly saw men performing it. So I was a little worried. But then I realized there's so much range to this character, Ariel is dramatically so flexible. I just saw Ariel as airy, whereas Caliban is earthy. Ariel is light, and fire, and Caliban is earth and wood.

Q: HOW DID THAT INSIGHT IMPACT YOUR PERFORMANCE? HOW DOES ONE BEGIN TO TRANSLATE THOSE CHARACTER TRAITS INTO A PERFORMANCE?

A: I think it's in everything she does – it's even in the costuming. With Shakespeare, it's the words, of course, but once I got the words down, I think the costume help put it all together. I felt so huge with my costume, especially in the "You three are men of sin" scene. I felt so much lager than my five foot, two inch frame!

Q: Can you describe the costume?

A: It was a mish-mash. I knew that we were going to have costumes given to us, but I was also kind of worried. What are they going to come up with? I thought maybe I should start looking at stuff on my own. And I just happened to find this black dress with sequins on it, which I thought was pretty interesting. It wasn't from the time period, but I thought maybe I should just hang on to this. And then this store happened to be selling Halloween costumes early, so I found this "Dark Angel" costume, and I was enamored of the wings. I thought "That is Ariel." So I got it. Then I just kind of built on that. The black feathers were supplied to me, as well as the mask. And piece by piece, it just fell together. It was hot behind the mask, but I felt huge, like there was no limit to this character.

Q: What are the adjectives you would use to describe the character of Ariel?

A: Well, Prospero calls her, "My tricksy spirit." She's very tricksy – and magical. She's ethereal, but also terrifying, as with the storm. There's a range – she's not just in a box. She can be fragile, but then grow. She's not human, so you can kind of make her anything you want. As an actor, that's kind of freeing.

# John Kuhn

**"** *There's the beauty of Shakespeare – you reach the level of art, you reach the level of language being used to shape and express a thought that is done in a way that is unique and beautiful.* **"**

*John Kuhn graduated from The Ohio State University in 1983 with an MFA in Acting, then taught acting and directing for over 28 years at various institutions including Oberlin College, The University of Toledo and The University of Michigan-Flint. Off-Broadway and regional stage work includes -"El Gallo" in The Fantasticks for CATCO, "Oberon" in A Midsummer Night's Dream for the Virginia Arts Festival, and "Chuck" in The Ha Ha Club, New York Theatre Fringe Festival. Independent film work includes- "Manager" in Brotherly Love (aired on PAX and WGN), "Jason Frothingham" in Mrs. Stevens Hears the Mermaids Singing, and "Connor Lumford" in The Endangered, selected for The Hollywood Black Film Festival.*

*Directing projects include The Crucible for Gallery Players (with Maggie Grace), ANNA WEISS for Red Herring Theatre Company, As You Like It and Hamlet for Actors' Theatre Company of Columbus, and Half Full... of It for the 2005 Toronto Theatre Fringe Festival.*

*He is, currently, Artistic Director of Actors' Theatre Company of Columbus and pursuing his PhD at OSU.*

Q: Do you remember the first time you read, or saw, Shakespeare?

A: My family didn't attend theatre. I didn't have a theatre-going tradition at all. It was a fluke I stumbled into this art form. The first memory I have of Shakespeare – probably what most students have – is an English class. A pretty traditional setting. We sat and read from the plays – it was in high school, sophomore or junior year. There might have been a brave soul to read it aloud, but mostly we just read it to ourselves. My memory is it was daunting. It was hard as heck to figure out what was being discussed, given the use of a lot of different poetic elements that I was unfamiliar with. It was extremely challenging figuring out the meaning. On the other side, there were those pearls of expression that have become well known, and which are almost too poetic to be expressed. So I went back and forth between thinking "Oh my gosh, what does that mean?" to "Oh my gosh, that's beautiful!" I remember just being daunted. I was intimidated by the language even as I was being overwhelmed by the power and beauty of language. Both extremes.

Q: How did you get involved with theatre?

A: The end of my junior year I sort of stumbled into it. I was in a concert chorale. One of my friends came in and said they needed guys in the chorus for *Bye Bye Birdie*. No acting required. Because he was my friend, I agreed. I had no experience at that time – but

I loved it! I found that I really enjoyed that communication across the stage, my camaraderie with other actors…it was thrilling.

Q: Do you remember the next shows you were in?

A: *The Man Who Came to Dinner,* and *Pippin* – and I also auditioned at a Catholic girls' school – they did *Kiss Me Kate.* That was senior year, and then I went right from there into a BFA program. Once I got into this area, I knew it was what I wanted to pursue.

Q: What school did you attend?

A: Southwest Missouri State – I was accepted into their BFA program. And that's where I had my first experience performing Shakespeare, and also other period pieces, such as the *Duchess of Malfi,* a revenge tragedy very much along the kinds of language elements Shakespeare uses – a very powerful piece, a great character study. I performed in that first, and that whetted my appetite to perform Shakespeare. The first play of his I did was *Twelfth Night.* I was Malvolio.

Q: Pretty challenging part -- what was that experience like?

A: There was something special about doing that show, about working with a director who guided me through the role. *Twelfth Night* is more accessible than many of Shakespeare's other works. Working with a really good director helped hone my appreciation and understanding of what Shakespeare was doing with language.

From then on, I've always enjoyed doing Shakespeare, both as an actor and as a director.

Q: DO YOU THINK SOME ACTORS ARE INTIMIDATED BY THE LANGUAGE, AND NEVER REALLY GET COMFORTABLE WITH THE LINES, OR EVEN KNOW WHAT THEY ARE SAYING?

A: After I went to OSU, I went out to teach. I've been the head of a couple of BFA programs, and I felt it was important that students have that experience of these rhetorical elements, that they know how to shape a speech so that it builds. That kind of rhetorical thinking – we don't engage in much anymore. But actors need to be adept at how to be persuasive, how to make their points. That's what Shakespeare and writers of that period were doing. They had been taught since grammar school how to make a point, how to use rhetorical tools to persuade.

Q: WHAT ARE THE EXPERIENCES YOU'VE HAD IN YOUR WORK WITH SHAKESPEARE THAT HAVE MADE THE BIGGEST IMPRESSION ON YOU?

A: Well, I've had a lot of experience as an actor and as a teacher. One of my most profound experiences happened in 1986. I knew some of the teachers at Oberlin College – they were creating a summer theatre institute. They wanted to bring in a couple of British actors, and then hire some American teachers, and we'd put on classes during the day and also present productions. One of the greatest experiences for me was Patrick Stewart was brought in to play Prospero. I was cast as Antonio – a hugely eye-opening experience. Patrick Stewart was such a consummate professional – he not only knew stage craft but the handling of the language. It was like a graduate course.

Prior to this, he had done a number of things in theatre, with the RSC, and some films, but he didn't yet have the name recognition he would soon have with *Star Trek: The Next Generation*. The stage presence he brought to the roles he embodied was impressive. And I remember he was out there playing soccer with the kids, kicking the ball around. He was in great physical shape, and that sense of keeping your instrument fit – because Shakespeare is demanding, in terms of breath control, and physical demands – that was a lesson I think I learned from him.

Q: WHAT OTHER LESSONS HAS YOUR WORK IN THEATRE TAUGHT YOU?

A: To continue studying! It's important in the field of acting that one doesn't stop developing. I tend to take a pretty eclectic approach, largely informed by Stanislavski, so the more I know the more effective I can be. The more I know, the more I can share, and help the young developing actor find the tools and techniques they need.

There's a really marvelous Eastern philosophy concept I use in terms of how I approach teaching: I want the student to stand on my shoulders, to go beyond whatever I've been able to discover, to grow beyond that. The only way I can help that happen is to continue my process as well. We've all encountered instructors who had their energy, their flash, their enthusiasm years ago, and now it's just a job. Often a passionless job. Think of the word amateur, which comes from the root of "to love." It's often a danger to lose that "love of." I try to embody both the amateur element of loving it, as in the true amateur sense, as well as bringing an element of professionalism

Q: How did you become Artistic Director of Actors' Theatre of Columbus?

A: Because I was teaching, and including classical plays, I had a pretty strong background in that type of theatre. When we moved to Columbus, I auditioned with Actors' Theatre of Columbus, and also directed for them. The artistic director at that time was moving on, taking a position at Northwestern, and he suggested I apply, and I did. And I got it. It's been a marvelously rewarding experience. Also frustrating – our budget is not huge. As a non-profit, we're constantly struggling to find the funds we need to do what we do. But we've been around for a while, and we're given a huge amount of support from the community.

It started out as very much an amateur community theatre. People would get into costume at somebody's house, walk over to the park, perform, and then walk home. But we've expanded over the years to where we are now doing several different productions each summer.

Q: That kind of commitment from amateur actors is impressive. What is it, do you think, that drives certain people to perform?

A: It operates on a number of different levels. Some of it is simply the fun of doing a show, the camaraderie of coming together, as a family. Hopefully, you continue these relationships, though often that doesn't happen. You go back to your lives. So some of it is relationship. Some of it is the sense of accomplishment. As anyone involved in theatre knows, it takes a lot of time and effort. But once you have been involved in a production, that sense of "Wow, we did this! We affected all these people, and it was appreciated!" – applause is something that's really potent.

Q: Is that especially true, do you think, with performing Shakespeare? Are the satisfactions greater?

A: I think, regarding Shakespeare, Harold Bloom says it best when he talks about how our understanding of what it means to be human comes from Shakespeare, from the characters he explores in his plays. So much of our understanding of motivation, why we act the way we do, comes from his writing. So when you perform him, you're learning, you're growing.

And then there's the beauty of Shakespeare – you reach the level of art, you reach the level of language being used to shape and express a thought that is done in a way that is unique and beautiful. When you work as an actor, you get to say those words out loud. For a brief moment on stage, you all get to embody those words, and pretend that they are your words. That's exciting.

Q: What about the satisfactions of being Artistic Director?

A: One of my early experiences as Artistic Director – I was doing *A Midsummer Night's Dream*, and we're rehearsing outside, and we have people walk by all the time, watching what we are doing. And we were rehearsing the play within the play, and these kids were riding their bikes, and they just stopped, and they're spread out around the stage, and they're just leaning on their handlebars, kids from the neighborhood, different ethnicities, and they just stayed there for fifteen, twenty minutes, just watching. These are kids just riding their bikes, having fun, and they just stayed there, watching us rehearse. That potential for impacting young lives with a presentation about what it means to be human...to bring that to an audience is my passion and why I love doing what I do.

Q: DO YOU PREFER ACTING OR DIRECTING?

A: It varies. I really enjoyed doing Shylock last year. I did that in the summer, and I did Oberon in *A Midsummer Night's Dream*. I did Atticus Finch in *To Kill a Mockingbird*, and then I did Hector in *The History Boys*. Very meaty roles – in two of them I was a director, two of them, I was an actor. They are very different hats to wear. Serving as a director is fun, but there's a lot of enjoyment as well in just being an actor and honing in solely on one character.

Q: WHEN YOU DIRECT, DO YOU EVER GET GOOD SUGGESTIONS OR INSIGHTS FROM AMATEUR CAST MEMBERS?

A: Oh yeah. Oh yeah. For example, one of my Dromios [in *Comedy of Errors*] has a real strong comic vein as an actor. He commits one-hundred percent to his role, even in the rehearsal process. A lot of my work with him, for example, wasn't necessarily offering specific direction It was more guiding him through *his* choices. It wasn't like telling him "Do this." It was more helping him fine tune his performance. Every actor is different.

Q: IS IT HARD TO GET A MASS AUDIENCE TO COME TO A SHAKESPEARE PLAY, AS OPPOSED TO SOMETHING "LIGHTER" OR LESS CHALLENGING?

A: One of the things I do as artistic director is try to offer a range of plays. Audience attitudes and interests change over time. You're constantly trying to find what types of plays will be most accessible or generate the most interest. For the last few years, we've been using as our big season opener these big swashbucklers – *Robin Hood, King Arthur, The Three Musketeers* – plays with romance, sword fighting, lots of action. We have found it helps get people in, establish the habit of going to see a play. That's been our approach.

With all that said, we have a very loyal and large contingent that just comes out for the Shakespeare. We tend to do mainly the comedies and tragedies, rather than the histories. But we have a very loyal audience. Last Sunday, there was a family there that had been coming for twenty years. It's outdoors, they come every year, spread out a blanket. It was great to get a sense of how much they appreciated our presence in their lives.

Q: SHAKESPEARE'S BEEN A PRESENCE IN YOUR LIFE FOR MANY YEARS. WHAT HAVE YOU GOTTEN FROM HIM?

A: I think a richer appreciation and understanding of life. You can't help but take something from that immersion and that exploration of his work, you can't help being shaped and changed by that. Thoughts and words have power. We are affected by the words we use to shape our thoughts, and if indeed that's what occurs, it's even more important that we go to those sources that have the richest, deepest, most profound thoughts available. And for me, the thoughts and the language of Shakespeare have deepened my ability to conceptualize about everything. He's such a universal playwright – his plays deal with it all: what does it mean to love? What does it mean to seek revenge? I feel like I am a better person – more understanding, more knowledgeable – because of my work with Will.

# Seth Meriwether

*" The works are classics, really. Hundreds of thousands of people have performed him, and each one has taken the text in a different direction. "*

*Seth Meriwether was born in Montgomery, Alabama on April 19th, 1995. He started acting around the 4th grade and it has become his passion ever since. Seth is an avid outdoorsman, writer, photographer, aspiring pilot, musician, backpacker, and with his adventurous and curious mindset every new challenge interests him. He enjoys being well rounded not only in the business side of his life, acting, but also in his day-to-day life. Seth, the son of Nick and Kelly Meriwether, feels that real world experiences help shape and form his characters later on, and it just keeps life interesting.*

Q: WHAT WAS YOUR FIRST ENCOUNTER WITH SHAKESPEARE?

A: It was *Twelfth Night* – at a camp I went to at the Alabama Shakespeare Festival when I was eleven. You spend the whole week designing costumes, blocking your scenes, working with a group. Each group does a reduced scene. It was so cool being wrapped up in all that stuff – seeing what happens, the magic that happens behind the scenes. That was my first show. I loved being animated, getting up there and pretending. That's all acting is – pretending.

I remember the sword fight. We didn't have real swords, we used wrapping paper rolls wrapped in duct tape. It was very cool being able to do that – every kid loves to sword fight. After that, I was approached by someone from the Shakespeare Festival. They wanted me to get involved in their program for young performers.

My fourth grade teacher – I give her all the credit for getting me started. We had these skits in class. We were all dressed up as Indians and had to come up with like a campfire chant. Apparently, she saw something in our skit. They brought the other classes in to watch. My teacher signed me up for the scholarship to go to the camp, which I wouldn't have done otherwise.

Q: DO YOU THINK YOUR EARLY EXPOSURE HELPED YOU GET COMFORTABLE WITH SHAKESPEARE, AND THE DIFFICULTIES OF HIS LANGUAGE?

A: Well, with Shakespeare, it can get confusing because of the language. In *Richard III*, when I was in sixth grade, I played the Duke of York. I remember going in for my costume fittings, getting to wear this great hat, and doublet. That was the coolest thing. I remember they had two shows running where we performed, and we'd see the other actors between acts, and I thought it was really cool to see other actors up close, behind the scenes. I didn't know what the language meant but there were people who helped us break it down, give us a sense of what the words mean. I remember the director said "Let's be professional about this and help these people watching this play" – that stuck with me, the value of performing, and what you can bring to an audience, how important it was to perform as well as you can for the audience. There was one part we got to be ghosts – what kid doesn't like to be a ghost? We had our faces painted white and got to haunt Richard. It was great fun!

That was my first professional show, but I did Shakespeare camps, and I did *The Tempest* during a week-long camp. I had also done competitions in high school, and in-class stuff where you do Shakespeare speeches. I did Richard's "Now is the winter" speech. And in junior high, I did *The Complete Works of Shakespeare (abridged)*. They didn't have a drama club when I started there, and we had this meeting, and they said "Who wants to be president of the Drama Club?" and I was like, "I'll be president." They said "What kind of show should we do?" and I remember having seen *The Complete Works of Shakespeare,* and it was really funny. So we did it, and I just sort of directed it, just working through the scenes.

Q: So you had some experience with Shakespeare, but the language must have been a challenge for your classmates.

A: Yes! They hadn't really had any intro to Shakespeare, and had no background on his works. The text was completely new to them, so there were some troubles at first. I had a bit more background, and once we all went through it, talked about it, we were able to carry through successfully.

Q: When did you decide on pursuing theatre seriously?

A: Really, after that first show, *Richard III.* Acting is so much fun – you get paid to be someone else.

Q: HAVE YOU READ OTHER SHAKESPEARE PLAYS — ONES YOU HAVEN'T PERFORMED IN?

A: Oh sure. I remember reading *Henry V.* I was interested in all the intrigue of the kings and queens of the time period.

Q: HOW ABOUT WATCHING SHAKESPEARE BEING PERFORMED?

A: Oh yes. When we did *Twelfth Night,* the day we got done with that show, our version, they did a professional production of the same show. That was really great seeing what they did with the same show.

Q: DO YOU REMEMBER SEEING ANY MOVIES VERSIONS OF SHAKESPEARE — AND WAS THAT HELPFUL IN SOME WAY?

A: Back in the seventh grade I saw the film of *Romeo and Juliet,* and I remember we watched the Mel Gibson *Hamlet* in seventh grade. I just recently watched the newer version of *Hamlet*...that gave a lot of insight to me as an actor. I love to watch a great actor pick apart a character.

Q: YOU'VE DONE BOTH FILM AND STAGE WORK. HOW DO THEY DIFFER?

A: This is just for me, but in theatre you can be really sincere, and you're tugging the audience's heart and you feel connected. You can hear a pin drop, but you still have to be loud, volume-wise and movement-wise so they can see you. And the rehearsal period is different. You do it every night, over and over. In film, there might not be any rehearsal at all. Your rehearsal is your take. You show up, hit your spot, and just go. With film, you can bring your voice down. You don't have to be loud to make your point. You might have a camera five inches from your face, but you still have to have the same focus, the same intensity.

Q: Which is more challenging?

A: I wouldn't say either one is more difficult. Obviously, memorizing lines and getting into character are always a challenge, transferring what's on a page into a real character. They are equally difficult once you get your mind wrapped around it. Being able to make changes in film on the spot is important – a director might tell you after your take, "I want you to try it THIS way," and you have to be able to change. And of course, there's a lot of competition in both of them.

Q: Which is more satisfying?

A: I suppose theatre, if you look at it as a whole. All the things that have to work to pull it off, night after night – that's satisfying. With film it changes day to day. But personally for me, film is satisfying because you can watch your end result. And with film you can see what you've done, and what the effect is on people, in terms of box office. But I still love both.

Q: Why do you think Shakespeare is still so popular today?

A: His works are timeless. If you look at the way he wrote, and look at all the other authors who were also writing at that time, you read Shakespeare and say "How did he come up with *this way* of saying that?" That's what draws us to him – the works are classics, really. Hundreds of thousands of people have performed him, and each one has taken the text in a different direction. There's a timelessness…you can adapt it to any time, almost any interpretation. The way he wrote makes him the best of the best.

Q: WHAT DOES THE FUTURE HOLD FOR YOU, AS A PERFORMER?

A: As an actor, you never know. But I have great agents, and I feel I've been dealt a great hand. This fall, I plan on going to school, and then hopefully going to L.A. and making it in film. I've been fortunate enough to find work while I'm here, but L.A. has kind of always been a dream of mine. I don't want to be that guy who says "I was a an actor in my teens, but now I have to get *serious.*" I don't want to NOT pursue it. I want to give it a shot and do what I love. If I'm living off of Spam and water, well, that's what I'll do. Whatever it takes.

# Noelle Fair

> **"** *The easiest thing about it is the Iambic beats replicate the heartbeat. It's the simplest human rhythm within us. We just tend to ignore it, and that type of human exposure to the heart that Shakespeare makes us feel is frightening for many actors.* **"**

*Noelle Fair grew up in Gaithersburg, Maryland where she started pursuing theatre at a young age, taking classes at Bethesda Academy of Performing Arts and Round House Theatre School. She did many high school and community theatre plays in her area and eventually pursued a bachelor's degree in Acting at Towson University in Baltimore, Maryland. While at Towson, Noelle worked with Baltimore Shakespeare Festival (Julius Caesar, 2004) and had an internship with the National Theatre Workshop of the Handicapped (Belfast, ME). After college Noelle moved to NYC in order to pursue acting. During her five years there, she appeared in many shows throughout the city, Off- Broadway, and regional productions. Noelle recently completed her Master's in Staging Shakespeare at the University of Exeter in Devon, England. Through this program Noelle attended the Shakespeare's Globe Education Residency program twice where she received classes in movement, voice, stage combat, and historical dance.*

*She is the Resident Teaching Artist for Hudson Shakespeare Company , which she helps to run alongside her husband, Jon. Outside of the-*

*atre Noelle likes to play sports such as volleyball and martial arts. She also loves to travel and hopes to be able to explore the world with her husband.*

Q: WHEN DID YOU FIRST ENCOUNTER SHAKESPEARE? AND WHAT KIND OF IMPRESSION DID IT MAKE ON YOU?

A: I first encountered Shakespeare in my eighth grade English class. We were reading *As You Like It,* which is not usually one that is touched upon in schools (although in my opinion, should be). Our teacher went through this play as slowly as anything I've ever done. She never wanted us to read it at home, because she wanted us to take our time going through it. She also believed that Shakespeare was meant to be performed. She would have students get up in front of the class to act out scenes. After almost every sentence she would stop and say "What does that mean?" The class would find an answer, then she would have the student act the line out again with that meaning. After we had finished the reading of the play, we modernized scenes and performed them for the class. As a finale to this whole thing, she took us down to the National Theater in DC to see a performance of *As You Like It* with Kelly McGillis as Rosalind. I understood every word. I was also able to see the fun in it, and the joy others had with it. I remember distinctively the audience having a huge reaction of shock after Orlando's line "There was no thought of pleasing you when she was christened." At the time, I didn't quite get the joke or why it was funny, so I was aware there was still something about the language that I didn't understand, but from that performance, I knew I wanted to continue to crack the code to understanding and enjoying Shakespeare.

Q: Did you perform Shakespeare in high school, either in a classroom or on stage? What do you remember about that experience?

A: A little bit of both actually. In the classroom, I do remember performing scenes from Shakespeare's plays. Specifically, I remember going over to a friend's house to film a scene from *Othello* where I played Emilia. Other then that, my performance experiences in the classroom were limited to reading scenes and trying not to be an actor so as to fit in with kids who otherwise didn't care about performing or learning. My junior year of high school I was cast in a production of *Midsummer Night's Dream* as Quince. What I remember about that experience was that I had a fun time with the other mechanicals, and I think we had an easier time of it than the lovers or fairies as most of our language was prose. I remember one of the most frustrating parts of the role was Quince's Prologue speech "If we offend, it is with our good will." I got so overwhelmed with it that I think I broke down during one of our final rehearsals. I just could not understand it, and I could not communicate it, let alone remember it. My director came to me and said "I know why you're having problems with it. It was written to be bad. Play it like a bad actor." I also remember loving the larger prologue speech where he says "With blade, with bloody blameful blade, he bravely broached his boiling bloody breast." I was so tickled by the sentence, by the sounds, by the consonance. It was my favorite piece of text to say every night.

Q: When did you get interested in performing, in general? Was there anyone who was influential in your interest in performing?

A: I got interested in performing sort of by accident. I was eight years old and was having a sleep over at a friend's house. My friend's mother informed me that her daughter regularly went to an acting class on Saturday mornings, and that I would probably need to come along the next morning as a guest. I guess my mother agreed. Acting class was fun. We played imaginary games for a few hours, then went to the local Mrs. Fields and got a hot chocolate chip cookie on on our way out. (Who wouldn't like it?) On the way out, the teacher caught my mother and said "I think your daughter enjoys this" and so my mother signed me up for the class. I took a class following the initial one at the same studio (Bethesda Academy of Performing Arts in Bethesda, Maryland) for a few weeks and at the end of it, we had an evaluation. I remember my evaluation said something like "I recommend Noelle takes the next level of this class" and again, another teacher was verbally talking to my mother and telling her I seemed to enjoy myself and said "She has a knack for this." I guess it wasn't any one thing, but from a very early age, I had tapped into something, and felt encouraged, and that level of encouragement felt good. I wasn't sure what I was doing, but I was very aware at that time, that somebody was giving me positive praise for something, and it felt like encouragement towards something I should be doing for the rest of my life.

Q: WHAT SHAKESPEAREAN ROLE HAVE YOU MOST ENJOYED PLAYING? WHAT ARE THE SHAKESPEARE ROLES YOU'D LIKE TO PLAY THAT YOU HAVEN'T?

A: I really enjoyed playing Regan from *King Lear.* I was not too familiar with the show or role at the time, so I loved discovering the part for the first time. I found it liberating to take on a role which didn't have any baggage attached to it as well. I could just concentrate on my own interpretation of the part and do what I felt was genuinely happening in the moment. It was also fun doing the eye-gouging scene! I would love to play Rosalind from *As You Like It,* and Viola from *Twelfth Night,* and after my last Globe residency I got a taste of Paulina from *Winter's Tale* (I performed the infamous trial scene) and so I am chomping at the bit to play this role. Before I get too old, I'd also like to tackle Marina from *Pericles.*

Q: DO YOU PREPARE DIFFERENTLY TO PERFORM SHAKESPEARE THAN YOU WOULD FOR THE WORK OF ANOTHER, MORE MODERN PLAYWRIGHT?

A: Yes, I actually do prepare differently. I think you have to. Shakespeare's language is like a puzzle and once you take time to figure out the pieces, only then can you put them back together in order to use it. Firstly, I break down the meter. I go through my text marking out the iambic pentameter. I also take note of the type of meter it is. Is my character speaking in prose? Why? Do they switch to verse, and why do they switch? What is happening? Giles Block, the Text Coach at Shakespeare's Globe has a great way of looking at prose. He says when a character is in prose, they are hiding something. A great example of this is Beatrice from *Much Ado About Nothing.* For most of the show, she speaks in prose. Then, when she switches to verse it is when she declares her love for Benedick after overhearing her cousin. The entire time prior to this declaration she has been hiding the fact that she is harboring her feelings of love towards Benedick. Moments such as this are important to notice. Additionally, if a character is in prose and then switches to verse within the context of the scene could also mean something important to you as an actor.

Q: WHAT SPECIAL CHALLENGES DO SHAKESPEARE'S LANGUAGE POSE FOR AN ACTOR?

A: Often I have heard actors who typically do more modern based work say "I DON'T DO SHAKESPEARE – I don't get it, I don't understand it." In my head, they are afraid of it, and unwilling to do the work needed in order to unravel the pieces of the puzzle. In today's society, I find we do not use the depth of language that Shakespeare does in our every day life. I'm not trying to say that the every day conversation in Elizabethan times was highly poetic or that Shakespeare was somehow replicating every day speak – but that there was more of an appreciation for poets, and for the work of poets. We don't have patience any more to dissect this text. I think modern actors find it intimating and overwhelming. I think they are not understanding some essential elements which make him fun and relatable – Shakespeare is highly raunchy, and the easiest thing about it is the Iambic beats replicate the heartbeat. It's the simplest human rhythm within us. We just tend to ignore it, and that type of human exposure to the heart that Shakespeare makes us feel is frightening for many actors, and I think we're disconnected from it. All in all, I'd say we don't trust it

Q: WHY DID YOU PURSUE A RESIDENCY WITH SHAKESPEARE'S GLOBE? WHAT DOES THAT INVOLVE, SPECIFICALLY?

A: In order to fully understand how to stage the plays for a modern audience, we need to fully understand the original contexts and playhouses for which the plays were written. It is many scholars belief that playwrights write for the buildings their plays will be performed in, so consequently, this indicates that Shakespeare, who worked mostly in the Globe would have written his plays to work in that building with the present conditions concerning open air space, audience interaction, running time of shows, and playing space conditions of actors.

Q: ARE THERE DIFFERENCES IN THE WAY AMERICAN ACTORS AND BRITISH ACTORS APPROACH/PERFORM SHAKESPEARE?

A: If you had asked me last year, I probably would have said yes, being new to the UK, but now I'm inclined to say no. I think it's a big fallacy to say the British approach or perform it differently than Americans. I think what this does to Americans is makes them feel inferior: that somehow we can't manage the language or tackle it with dexterity, clarity, wit, and understanding. I found this not to be true.

Q: ARE THERE DIFFERENCES BETWEEN THE WAYS AMERICAN AND BRITISH AUDIENCES RESPOND TO SHAKESPEARE?

A: Again, I don't think so. In both cultures I have met three kinds of people – those who want nothing to do with the man or his plays, those who can go to a play and get the general sense of what is happening and enjoy it, and those who love the plays and are obsessed.

Q: DO YOU HAVE A FAVORITE SHAKESPEARE FILM? AND WHAT MAKES IT SO?

A: In regards to Shakespeare films, I tend to be something of a Kenneth Branagh fan. I like his zeal and bombastic risky nature. He attacks the text with speed, clarity, and specificity. I think a lot of actors go about Shakespeare in generalities, in broad swaths of thoughts, and I tend to like his work because he doesn't do that.

Q: FINALLY, WHAT DO YOU THINK IS THE SECRET TO SHAKESPEARE'S ENDURING POPULARITY?

A: There's a book called *Shakespeare: The Invention of the Human* by Harold Bloom – who, brilliant as he is, is judgmental and crass and I find his verbiage annoying to read. However, he says that the idea with Shakespeare is "that Shakespeare's understanding of the human creature; the nature of our lives as human creatures, combined with Shakespeare's preternatural artistic gifts has actually changed our understanding of what it is to be human." Prior to this, plays were not that popular. There were court Masques and traveling play companies, or morality plays and cycle plays, but this writer, for the first time, put the human experience and what it means to be alive, and put it down on paper for us to hear. I think we still find Shakespeare's words relatable to our own times, I think we constantly see and feel his relevancy in our lives. I think we like to be pioneers in our field, so by venturing into a Shakespeare play, you are hoping to make new discoveries and then share those discoveries with others. I think we're trying to understand him and find out who Shakespeare really was through his plays.

# Jay Tilley

*" I discovered that each Shakespeare production got easier over time. Shakespeare really kinds of lays it all out for you – you have some flexibility, some freedom, but he really lays it all out there. "*

*Jay Tilley has been appearing on stage around the Washington, DC area in a variety of productions with various community, dinner and profession-al theatre companies since 1999 and has dabbled in some local TV, film and voiceover work as well. Jay's Shakespeare credits include Romeo and Juliet (Friar Laurence), The Taming of the Shrew (Petruchio), and Julius Caesar (Brutus). Other notable stage credits include The Odd Couple (Oscar Madison), Frankenstein (Victor Frankenstein), and Capone (Al Capone - solo performance).*

*Jay has been honored for some of his performances. He was most recently awarded Maryland Theatre Guide's Reader's Choice Award for Best Lead Actor in a Play for The Odd Couple. He also received a Reston Community Players or "Restie" award for Best Character Actor for As You Like.*

*He can currently be seen in the award-winning web series Shotgun Mythos (James Saylor) and is a regular performer in ComedySportz improv shows at The Comedy Spot in Arlington, VA.*

*Jay studies journalism at USC and now, by day, works for a healthcare market research firm near DC. He and his wife wife Melissa (who is also heavily involved in the DC area theatre community) live in Manassas, VA with their two dogs Gwen and Morgan.*

Q: WHAT WAS YOUR FIRST ENCOUNTER WITH SHAKESPEARE?

A: I think my first memory was the Zeffirelli movie of *Romeo and Juliet*. Actually, when I was real small, my parents had an LP, the soundtrack from that film, you know "A Time for Love" – I was told I was singing from a very early age, two or three years old. I always loved music. Then when I saw the movie, I remembered it.

Q: DO YOU REMEMBER TACKLING SHAKESPEARE IN SCHOOL?

A: Reading Shakespeare's *Romeo and Juliet* in school I found incredibly boring. Then when I saw the movie, I thought it was really great. It might have been as early as seventh or eighth grade. I remember *Macbeth*. That wasn't boring. I had some teachers that tried to make it a little bit fun. We'd act it out. That was good. But the analyzing it, writing papers on it, that wasn't too exciting. I wasn't that interested in that approach to it. Acting it out is always better.

Q: DID YOU KEEP AT IT IN COLLEGE?

A: At the University of South Carolina, I was a journalism major. I didn't really get into Shakespeare, or theatre in college. I was much more into singing. It wasn't until after college that I really started getting into acting. I wanted to be more than a singer who acted. I wanted to be an actor who sang.

One of the first things I remember after college: I spent a couple of years in Arizona [working at a newspaper]. I was with a friend who also worked at the paper, and a Shakespeare company in Arizona did *A Comedy of Errors*. We went to see it, and it was a riot. They were all over the stage. It was a blast. They were great, and I remember thinking Shakespeare can be a lot of fun.

I started doing theatre in 1999. There were a couple of professional actors doing workshops at The Actors' Center, which is sort of a hub for actors in the DC area…they host workshops, have special events, and if you join, you can see shows in the area for a discount. So I went to a couple of these workshops. One of them was "Working with the First Folio." Another one was an introduction to the text, breaking it down, finding the proper rhythm.

I was trying to move into being more of an actor. Over the years, my first few years of being an actor, I encountered actors who had trained classically, knew what they were doing when it came to Shakespeare. I wanted to learn, get the technique to be able to perform Shakespeare well. I would meet these actors who had the technique, and I was very impressed. They taught me that if you can do Shakespeare, you can do almost any kind of acting. They give you a sharper technique, being able to pick out and communicate theme. So I knew I needed some classical training.

Q: WHEN DID YOU BEGIN PERFORMING SHAKESPEARE?

A: My first Shakespeare audition was for a group called Upstart Crow Productions. They put on quite a few shows. My audition was for *Richard II*, I think, back in 2002. I didn't do very well, wasn't really able to perform it well. What eventually ended up happening, after a couple more years of musicals, and a couple other plays, Upstart Crow had a lot of turnover. Some new people came in. A few people, though, stayed on, and my friend Heather called me and said they were going to do *Our Town*. She knew me, knew I'd be interested. I was cast as the Stage Manager. She said they were trying to re-launch Upstart Crow, do some more Shakespeare. She asked if I was interested, which I was. I was still doing mostly musical theatre at that time.

I went out for *Romeo and Juliet* and got cast as Friar Lawrence. For me, it was more difficult at first. What I found out over time, though, was that my musical theatre background helped me prepare. There's a music, a rhythm to his language. I think it definitely helped. Another thing that helped, Bob Smith, who directed me in a few other shows, an educator in the Fairfax County schools, he more or less taught me how to act Shakespeare. That was invaluable during rehearsal time. But I still had to breakdown the language, the stress, the rhythms. The way Bob liked to direct, when one scene was ending, another was already beginning – a very brisk pace. You go into it, thinking it was hard, but it really wasn't. I discovered that each Shakespeare production got easier over time. Shakespeare really kinds of lays it all out for you – you have some flexibility, some freedom, but he really lays it all out there.

Before I really started getting into Shakespeare, I had seen an interview with Kenneth Branagh, and they were talking to him about British actors versus Americans. He said, Americans are just as capable of doing it as Brits, but they are conditioned to think that they can't. And that's a shame, he said. But I think he's right – some Americans think it's too highbrow for us, but Shakespeare was writing for the common man. My director said "Put Shakespeare in the gutter where he belongs."

Q: WHAT'S THE MOST REWARDING PART OF PERFORMING SHAKESPEARE?

A: It's all rewarding, of course, but to be able to come out there and speak this beautiful language. It's just gorgeous. It seems really hard when you first consider it, but it's really not – it's almost easier because these lines have such a rhythm and poetry to them. And when you can tackle that, you feel you've accomplished something.

Q: WHAT HAVE YOU LEARNED FROM YOUR FELLOW ACTORS?

A: I'm constantly watching other actors to see what they're doing, to see what I can pick up. I think of all the things I've learned from them: proper diction, posture, breath support, the technical stuff – breaking down some of the symbolism, knowing when to hit a certain emotion. And knowing when to have more levels, go deeper, add more complication.

Q: WHAT SHAKESPEAREAN ACTORS DO YOU ADMIRE?

A: I really like – I know he's controversial but I really like Kenneth Branagh. He might not always use the "official" technique. He once said, "Once you learn the rules of Shakespeare, you can then unlearn them." Patrick Stewart does this – Kevin Kline, too. They make Shakespeare accessible. They make it seem so easy, kind of hip. What the cool kids are doing. I appreciate the fact that Branagh respects American actors, doesn't look down on them.

I saw a great production of *Taming of the Shrew* at the Shakespeare Theatre in DC. My favorite production of Shakespeare that I've seen there, maybe my favorite of all time, is *Titus Andronicus*. I have a friend who calls it the *Friday the 13th* of Shakespeare – very violent, bloody. But this production wasn't predictable. They mixed times: Ancient Rome and futurism. Just phenomenal. The feel and tone was great – better than a production of that play should be. I was blown away – it reminded me of why I like acting so much.

Q: HAVE YOU EVER THOUGHT ABOUT TRYING TO MAKE A LIVING AS AN ACTOR?

A: It would be nice to do it for a living – but I do it for the passion of it. If I ever win the lottery, maybe it will happen. Honestly, more than anything, I think it's luck. I've got a couple of actor friends working in the field, and they tell me it's `right place, right time.' Sometimes I think it's knowing the right person. I've seen performances here in community theaters that are just phenomenal, and I've thought "You should be on Broadway...you should be in Hollywood." There's a lot of things that have to fall in place.

Q: YOU PLAYED ORSON WELLES IN A ONE-MAN SHOW – WAS ANY OF YOUR SHAKESPEARE EXPERIENCE HELPFUL THERE?

A: He definitely had a Shakespearean quality to him – so great with language, words...great writer. You could argue that some of his life was Shakespearean, and his film career as well. He was a visionary who liked to push the envelope. The voodoo *Macbeth*, for example. Nowadays it's passe to put Shakespeare in a different time frame, but back then it was unheard of. As an actor, he could ham it up sometimes. He was sometimes guilty of playing Orson Welles rather than Shakespeare. If you watch his *Macbeth*, there's this one scene in particular, right after he meets the witches, he's playing himself, really chewing up the scenery. But he could also be just great.

Q: So Shakespeare poses a challenge for even the greatest actors?

A: A lot of actors are scared of Shakespeare. I was scared at first. But once I got those first few plays under my belt, it just made me want more. If I had my way, I'd do at least one Shakespeare production a year. Not only because it's fun to do, but it makes you a better actor. Every time I do a Shakespeare play, I come out of it a better actor. That's why I recommend every actor at least try.

# Colin Goode

*" When you're in the theatre, as a performer or even an observer, you're dealing directly with the big issues of life. I think the arts provide a necessary entry, and escape, into the essentials of life. Without getting too deep, I think God is an artist. I mean really, we're talking about the 'Creator.' "*

*Born in North of England 1937, with all the challenges of boyhood during WW2, Colin Goode grew up in a gloomy industrial town. While other boys kicked a ball around, Colin built model theaters. By age 11 he had lost both his parents. At age 13 he was invited to live in South Africa by an older sister who had emigrated after the war. High school in Johannesburg introduced Shakespeare into Colin's life and as a high school teacher he had the opportunity to direct school plays. He later launched a multi-media company producing documentary film and photography, in and around South Africa. His wife Moira was introduced to Shakespeare through visits to a delightful open air theater in Cape Town.*

*In 1976 Colin attended St John's College, Nottingham, UK to prepare for ordination as an Anglican Priest. He then spent the next 30 years working in South Africa, Canada, and the United States. In retirement he served as Vicar of Grace Church, Lopez Island, WA. In 2005 He and Moira established a fine arts gallery and studio on Lopez Island, where he paints and teaches landscape painting and Byzantine style iconography.*

Q: YOU ONLY RECENTLY BEGAN ACTING. WAS THE DESIRE TO PERFORM SOMETHING THAT WAS NEW IN YOUR LIFE?

A: I've always loved the theatre. I think I saw some other reality there, beyond my present experience. I got very involved with theatre when I was younger – I built model sets. In high school, I built a model of the Globe Theater.

Certainly my senior year was a pivotal one as far as Shakespeare. We did a detailed, intensive study of *Romeo and Juliet* in class. I got really involved in it. I was intrigued by it – and learned great chunks of the play. By the time I was 70 years old, when I finally performed the play, I actually still knew big chunks of the play. Surprisingly, I remembered it from all those years ago.

Q: SO WHY DIDN'T YOU PERFORM SOONER?

A: The chance to perform never seemed to materialize. My passion was to become a set designer in the theatre. But I took another way – I became a teacher.

I taught for four years – three years in a Johannesburg high school. Then I returned to England to teach in an English prep school. I was teaching English, and also some arts classes, fitting in wherever I could. When I went back to South Africa, I worked for a Christian youth organization, which ran summer camps for kids, which is what I did for nine years. I think some of my tendencies towards acting out came from that experience, where we did some wonderful things.

Then, I started a multi-media company in Capetown in the 1970s – prior to the advent of television, which didn't reach Capetown until 1978. I started a multi-media company – artists, photographers, and so on, and we made a few documentary films – financially we just couldn't make it. I was very involved with the church – I went to study theology in England for three years at 39, and was ordained as an Anglican priest at 42. Got a doctorate at a seminary in Pasadena, California – basically, the desire to teach has motivated me my whole career. I've also loved to paint – and I had wanted to open a gallery. Now I mainly paint, teach, and sell my own work – it's a mishmash.

Q: Did you have any connection throughout those years with Shakespeare?

A: When I was living in New York, I lived about five blocks from Lincoln Center, and I used to go to Shakespeare in the Park. I was the rector of a church called *All Angels* in Manhattan. We had quite a few people in our congregation who were actors. One show I particularly remember was *The Tempest* – with Patrick Stewart. The perspiration was kind of splashing on us – it had moved from the park to the theater. That was just a phenomenal production. And then on the occasions when I went back to England, I went back to Stratford. I saw a modern production of *The Merchant of Venice*, which didn't grab me as much. I personally like the plays as they were written, and the setting in which they were written. That's my choice when I go to see Shakespeare.

Q: How did you get involved with the Community Shakespeare Company of Lopez Island?

A: Richard Carter [founder and artistic director] is a remarkable person – he's worked with kids, very young kids, doing Shakespeare. He does that and he's also written adaptations of Shakespeare for children that have been widely used. It's amazing to see these little kids doing it. I went to these productions every year and then, in 2006, when he did *Romeo and Juliet*, he invited the adult members of the community to play some parts – and he invited me to audition for Friar Lawrence. Everything just came together – it was a wonderful production.

Q: WERE YOU AT ALL HESITANT TO AUDITION?

A: Well, I'm a hesitant person – I wasn't sure, at age seventy, if I could learn my lines. I thought "It's going to take me three weeks just to learn the first scene!" But the adrenaline flows, the momentum is generated, and you get into it. By the time the play was presented, I could probably have been a prompter without a script in front of me! I felt confident about the play. I was on a high with that. When I look back at the eleven years of being here, it was definitely a highlight. I've been in one other production – *The Laramie Project.* I played the Catholic Priest –I was typecast again! I'd like to try to do something else. I'd love to play all three witches – all myself.

When I came to Grace Church here to be a part-time vicar, I wasn't looking for a full time job. There was a theater attached to the church – wherever I've gone, there's always been a theatrical component.

Q: WOULD YOU SAY THE ARTS, IN GENERAL, HAVE ALWAYS BEEN IMPORTANT TO YOU?

A: When they advertised this position, it was part-time, and I thought this would give me a chance to establish a gallery. I was up front with them. It gave me the opportunity. In the ad, they were looking for someone who would blend in with the arts community. At that stage, I had decided to retire but I felt this was the place to come. And I came. I've got a lot of contact with people in the arts. It's wonderful.

When I played Friar Lawrence, a friend of mine came to me after the show and said "That was really good – you missed your vocation!" My head began to swell. I thought he was going to say "You should have been an actor." Instead, he said "You should have been a Franciscan friar!"

Q: You've read widely, performed theatrically, and you paint. Have you ever done any writing?

A: People have encouraged me to write over the years. I think I've waited too long to write. I don't have the recall I used to have. One of the reasons I don't do much preaching these days is I've had to keep pretty close to the script. It doesn't always make for vibrant preaching. There's an element of drama in preaching.

Q: Given what the arts have given you, do you have any thoughts on what can be done to instill a love of arts in younger people?

A: People like Richard Carter are the key to that – there's a great appreciation of the arts here. From where I live, I can see the whole community. There is a vibrancy about the arts here in this microcosm that is quite unique. And I think it's because there are key people who are enthusiastic about what they're doing. One of the things about Shakespeare is he deals in his plays with all the big issues of life. You've got anger, and deception, and love, and forgiveness, and hatred and reconciliation. All the big issues of life seem to be concentrated in the body of his work. When you're in the theatre, as a performer or even an observer, you're dealing directly with the big issues of life. I think the arts provide a necessary entry, and escape, into the essentials of life. Without getting too deep, I think God is an artist. I mean really, we're talking about the "Creator." In the Judeo-Christian idea, we are made in the image of our creator. And if we are made in that image, then there is that creative spirit in each of us. That love, that passion, that energy is what it means to be human. Without the arts, we're missing out on something truly essential.

Q: DO YOU THINK YOUNGER PEOPLE TODAY ARE MISSING OUT ON THAT? IS THERE TOO MUCH TIME AND ATTENTION BEING PAID TO SOCIAL MEDIA?

A: I think I'm an optimist by nature – I haven't entertained the possibility that we could be on the downward spiral on the arts. I would hope that social media could actually be a tool to enhance people's awareness and sensitivity about the arts. I'm not an authority about this, but the uprisings in certain parts of the world have been influenced strongly by social media. I know we're living in an age of small bites, but I think there is an urge in all of us to grapple with the larger issues, some of the deeper issues of life: why am I here? Where are we going? My experience is that it takes time for some of those realities to take hold. I would hope that in fact social media would be a means of getting people back into the arts which can help deal with those questions.

Q: When you were preparing for your role as the Friar, did you think about those larger issues? Or did you focus more on simply getting the lines down? How did you prepare?

A: Richard was a rich resource. I was constantly asking him, "Is this the right emphasis for this line?" or "How do I play this?" He was very good about using life experiences to help clarify how to approach certain aspects of the play. Other than Richard's help, I watched older productions on Netflix or at the library. That's how I learned.

One other thing: in the same year that I played Friar Lawrence, I went to a monastery in Cambridge, Massachusetts before we started rehearsals. The reason why is a parishoner encouraged me to write an icon. We think of "icon," and we think of the Greek for image, a two dimensional icon, like a painting. But in the business, people talk about "writing an icon," a two-way conversation. It's not an image – it's a window through which you approach God and God approaches you. And that's more akin to writing than painting. The icon I wrote was the Archangel Gabriel – I got into it. It met some needs for me that I was able to express. It's rather a detailed and prescribed process, but it appeals to that part of me. When I teach landscape painting, that's freer, looser. But iconography is more tightly controlled.

Q: Did that help you prepare for the role?

A: We spent the whole week in silence. There's not a lot of personal communication through what you are doing. I mean the problem with the part of Friar Lawrence is he offers the solution to Romeo and Juliet's problem, but he's also the cause of their disaster. He got it right in wanting to be helpful, and solve their problem, but there was a lack of communication. He had good intentions – there's the tragedy. But all is not lost. At the end, the Montagues and the Capulets are reconciled. I think Friar Lawrence's role is the critical one – he's the key to whether or not the whole thing works. And I think spending a week in the monastery was helpful. The brothers are very gracious and good people. Like Friar Lawrence, they have your best interests at heart.

# Lisa Stoeffel

*" When we put on a play, I feel like we fought a battle, and we were victorious. Somehow, we struggled and struggled, and against all odds, we came out and did a good job. "*

*Lisa Stoeffel grew up in London, England, and acted in a few high school plays. She decided to pursue a Fine Arts career before switching to advertising and commercial art. She worked in Atlanta and New York City for ten years, but left the corporate world to paint on commission at home. Her work has been exhibited and sold at the Montclair Art Museum in Montclair, New Jersey, and the Pioneer Art Museum in Woodward, Oklahoma.*

*Lisa holds a Post-Graduate Degree in Illustration and Graphic Design from The Portfolio Center in Atlanta, and received a Bachelor of Arts degree from Hollins University, Virginia, majoring in Studio Art and French. She worked as an Art Director, Graphic Designer and Illustrator at publishing companies in New York City and Atlanta. Freelance Illustration clients include The Montclair Public Library, McGraw-Hill, Inc., Prentice Hall Publishing, Atlanta Magazine, and The American Red Cross.*

*Lisa performs regularly with the St. James Players of Montclair.*

Q: WHAT IS YOUR FIRST MEMORY OF SHAKESPEARE?

A: First memory? Well, I grew up in London – was there from age six until I went to college, so Shakespeare was much more prevalent.

Q: WHAT TOOK YOU TO LONDON?

A: My father worked for Exxon. Well, back then it was Esso. Esso-Middle East. So he was over in Iran, and we got to stay in London, so I was in British schools, and we were reading Shakespeare as young as eight. It wasn't too fun at that point, because when you read it, you're not acting it. It's still kind of boring, and you can't figure out what it means. But growing up in London, you're kind of around Shakespeare. We would go to plays, and sometimes they were good, sometimes they were terrible – I mean, to a young girl. So I did have a lot of exposure to Shakespeare, but I didn't act any Shakespeare. I was in plays, but not Shakespeare.

Q: WOULD YOU SAY SHAKESPEARE IS SEEN DIFFERENTLY IN BRITAIN THAN IN AMERICA?

A: He's way more prevalent. Everybody knows Shakespeare. Way more prevalent...let me rephrase. While I was living there, my peers, everybody knew Shakespeare. You learned it in school, went to the plays. More people know about Shakespeare, and make the pilgrimage to go to Shakespeare's house at Stratford-upon-Avon.

Q: DID YOU MAKE THAT PILGRIMAGE?

A: Of course! My mother made us. And it was actually very cool. But nothing really impacted me about Shakespeare until I saw the movie "Shakespeare in Love." That sounds stupid. There I was living in London, going to the plays, visiting Stratford-upon-Avon, and learning all about him, but that movie just made it so real. I love that movie.

I would say in London, and in all of the south of England, Shakespeare is just more a part of the culture. You just absorb him, kind of by osmosis.

Q: TELL ME ABOUT THE CULTURAL RE-ADJUSTMENT YOU HAD TO MAKE WHEN YOU CAME TO THE U.S.

A: I went to school in Virginia, and I had a British accent – and I hated it! I just wanted to fit in, and there I was in the south. It was hard. All I wanted to do was to get back to London. It was a little difficult to assimilate, but once I did, everything was fine. America is great – Virginia is great. The weather is better, and the people are a lot more fun!

Q: WAS IT A WHILE BEFORE YOU RE-ENCOUNTERED SHAKESPEARE?

A: It definitely was. I don't remember reading any Shakespeare in college.

Q: Where did you go to college?

A: I went to Hollins College in Virginia. I was an art major and a French major, so I took a couple of English classes but not any Shakespeare. I wanted to be a famous painter. That was the plan. But then after graduation I realized you gotta eat. So then I went to learn how to be a graphic designer and illustrator, and I got into the advertising and illustration world. In all that time, I may have seen one Shakespeare play. Then, when we moved to New Jersey, we started to go to Shakespeare in the Park, you know, where you stand in line and get the free tickets. That's really fun, to see Shakespeare in Central Park.

Q: Do you remember any particular performances?

A: We went to see *As You Like It*, and we saw *Much Ado About Nothing*. But these were all professional productions, not amateur Shakespeare, so they of course spoke the language like it was real language. I learned from that – you have to just try to make it sound natural, like you're talking, not reciting iambic pentameter.

Q: When you perform Shakespeare, as you did in the recent production of *Twelfth Night*, you didn't sound like you were reciting it. You had a very natural delivery. Was that because you had paid attention to those actors, or was it due more to your British upbringing?

A: I don't know the answer to that, so maybe it's a combination. I thought it was important to have fun, so in our scenes, I was just trying to be natural. It felt like it was easier to say it as conversation than to recite it. And that's what Shakespeare was after, I think. And so it just kind of came naturally.

Q: Have you taken any acting classes?

A: Never. I had been in plays in high school, but not Shakespeare. And when we moved to Montclair [NJ], I got involved in doing puppet shows – putting on puppet shows in the schools, which is kind of like acting. And again, you have to speak really loudly and clearly and you're holding a puppet in front of you, and these puppets were almost the size of me. We were teaching kids about saying no to drugs, or about bullying, or how everybody is the same though we look different on the outside. Then, I directed a few things here [St. James Episcopal Church, Montclair]. I got involved in the youth group here, started leading it, and directed three Christmas pageants, led three ghost tours, then a Stations of the Cross play, and a Last Supper play.

Q: You volunteered to do this? Or were you drafted?

A: I started teaching Sunday school. I had been teaching for about sixteen years, and when I took on teaching the older students, that's when we decided to do plays, which the kids got excited about.

Q: Is that what led to your being in *A Midsummer Night's Dream*, the inaugural production of the St. James Players?

A: Yes, I got involved in the outreach committee, and met Tim Evans [Former Director of the St. James Players]. We had done some Bible study together. He came up to me and said "You have a lovely voice. Would you consider being Titania in *A Midsummer Night's Dream?*" and I said "Sure – how much work could that be?" That's how it started, as part of our outreach program to bring Shakespeare to less advantaged communities. I thought that was a really cool idea.

Q: TALK TO ME ABOUT THAT PRODUCTION.

A: It was our first one…I would say, overall, it was pretty good. There was some struggle with learning lines, but overall it was pretty successful.

Q: DID THAT PRODUCTION CHANGE, IN ANY WAY, HOW YOU FELT ABOUT SHAKESPEARE?

A: I would say it definitely made me want to learn even more about his works. So now I have a renewed interest in Shakespeare. I really do.

Q: HAS YOUR PERFORMANCE OF THE ROLES IN THE SHAKESPEARE PLAYS YOU'VE DONE —TITANIA IN *MIDSUMMER*, A GODDESS IN *TEMPEST*, AND MARIA IN *TWELFTH NIGHT* — IGNITED YOUR DESIRE TO TAKE ON, SAY, A LEAD ROLE LIKE LADY MACBETH?

A: I think I could do it. You think you could never memorize these lines, and then magically it happens. Geoffrey Rush says it's a mystery. You know, it just happens, but only after you go over them again and again and again. So I feel I could do it.

Q: HAS PERFORMING MADE YOU MORE INTERESTED IN READING THE PLAYS? REVISITING THE TEXTS?

A: I haven't really done that yet, but mostly because I keep finding all these other great books to read! I started reading *Game of Thrones*, and then I had to read every single book in the series. I loved them.

136

Q: A lot of actors I've spoken with say Shakespeare on the page just doesn't do it for them.

A: I agree. I think you need the people. The play needs the performers to make it come alive.

Q: Could that be why so many people think they don't like Shakespeare? Because they only know it through the texts they read in high school?

A: Yeah, I do think so. If they would just act one scene and be goofy, they'd find it so much more entertaining. Learning the speeches – that's good. There's use in memorizing the language. But if they acted it, you'd get some excitement going.

Q: So what do you think is the secret of Shakespeare's success?

A: He talked about themes that everybody understands: love, tragedy, identity. He was able to somehow find themes that were important in his own time – with lots of jokes and jibes at the political system and politicians of his day – but also to communicate something of lasting value. And his poetry is just gorgeous. People just don't find that kind of expression anywhere else.

Q: What do you get from performing? And what do you think art gives a person?

A: Deep questions. Well, I'm an artist so for me, art is an important part of my life. There's nothing I'd rather do than spend a day at an art museum. As far as the performing side of it, I really like the camaraderie of actors, the community of actors. If the community is not a good community, I wouldn't be interested in performing. When we put on a play, I feel like we fought a battle, and we were victorious. Somehow, we struggled and struggled, and against all odds, we came out and did a good job. Plus performing brings you out of yourself. If you're a shy person, you can pretend for a while to be really bold. If you're a serious person, you get to be goofy. You can explore different sides of yourself. You get in a zone that's no longer isolated, you're free to explore and create, and to play with different possibilities. Art creates those possibilities that might not seem possible in your regular life. I think Art is necessary because life can be difficult.

Q: I KNOW YOU ARE A PERSON OF FAITH. DO YOU SEE PERFORMANCE AS A KIND OF MINISTRY?

A: Absolutely. That's why I got involved in performing. Because it was outreach – we weren't preaching about God, but the people we performed for saw that we were with a church, and that we were out there trying to do good things in the community. God gives you the ability to act, to perform, and it's not good unless you can share it with somebody. It's like God is saying "Go out there and use your talent." You might not even be aware of the effect your work will have. Maybe there will be people in the audience who are like, "Wow, this is cool! Shakespeare isn't so boring after all!" And maybe they'll be motivated to get involved in community theatre. I think faith can motivate you to act, and then you get to share the good things that come from that with others.

# Matt Foss

**"** *I've learned to think of the audience as poets and geniuses. When you treat the audience that way, you can do a lot more. There is a rigor to our method, and audiences seem to get it.* **"**

*Matt Foss, assistant professor of acting and directing at the University of Idaho, received his MFA in Acting from Roosevelt University in Chicago and a PhD in Theatre Studies and Directing from Wayne State University in Detroit. Credits include Chicago Shakespeare Theatre, Oracle Theatre, Montana Shakespeare in the Parks, American Blues Theatre, The Jewish Ensemble Theatre and Tipping Point Theatre. Matt also performed and trained in Russia as a part of the American Studio of The Moscow Art Theatre School. In 2012 his production of SIX CHARACTERS at Iowa State University received the Kennedy Center's American College Theatre Festival's National Award for Outstanding Production of a Play and Outstanding Director of a Play. His student ensemble was recognized for Outstanding Lighting Design, three Distinguished Performance by an Actor awards, and citation for outstanding collaboration by a performance and production ensemble. He has worked extensively with both professional and amateur actors in a variety of venues.*

Q: DO YOU REMEMBER YOUR FIRST ENCOUNTER WITH
SHAKESPEARE?

A: Yeah, it was in high school. My junior year, my speech teacher gave us a scene from *A Midsummer Night's Dream*. I also remember we read *Romeo and Juliet*, and *Julius Caesar* in high school. After
we read it, I never touched it again.

Q: HOW ABOUT IN COLLEGE?

A: I went to Northwestern College – a small Christian liberal
arts school. The student body was conservative, but I had these really incredible professors. I learned how to write well – had some
really great teachers. But I never acted in a Shakespeare play there.
They had an incredible theatre program, and I did a ton of things
there, but I never did any Shakespeare. The most meaningful experience I had was when my biology professor asked me about
going to grad school. He said "What about theatre?" I guess he saw
something there.

So I went to Chicago – there are these cattle calls for all these
grad schools for MFA programs in theatre, and you go in and perform for two screeners – it's like *American Idol*. You audition at a
time slot, and then you come back two hours later, and you get a
letter that says yes, you can perform for all these schools, or no, you
didn't make the cut. I got a rejection letter. So I took it to Kinkos,
and I forged a letter that said I *could* be seen. There's like a box
that gets checked. I changed the "no" to "yes." And so I showed up
at the top floor of the Hilton Towers in Chicago, and had a hand-
ful of headshots and resumes, and I gave them each a packet with
all my stuff, and I even started doing my monologue right there in
the hallway, or in the hotel room or wherever I could. One school,
Roosevelt University, took a flyer on me.

Q: How did you get involved with Chicago Shakespeare?

A: I saw an announcement posted about auditions there so I went. Going to Chicago Shakespeare and auditioning and never having performed Shakespeare is like hearing a little bit about baseball and then going to try out for the New York Yankees. Well, after the piece I did, the casting director asked if I had anything else. I said yes, and I did something else from *Henry IV*. And then he asked, did I have anything else? And I said, yeah, and I did something from *The Tempest*. And he asked again, and I gave him a couple of non-Shakespeare monologues, and then eventually, I just starting improvising monologues, making them up on the spot. He told me later he had to cast me because he had never seen anyone make-up monologues before. I kind of had a master class there at Chicago Shakespeare, mostly listening to plays in the back of the theater, listening to some of the best actors in the city. Once in a while they put me in the plays, but mostly I'd just sit and listen.

Q: What was your next move?

A: I was recommended to Montana Shakespeare in the Parks, which is sort of the Triple-A for Chicago Shakespeare, and went out there to do summer Shakespeare. It was like boot camp. I didn't have any bad habits to unlearn. I was 22. After that, for the next 10 years, the majority of my work was in Shakespeare.

Q: Were you at all intimidated, or insecure, about doing Shakespeare with very little experience?

A: I just didn't really know any better – I didn't know how to act Shakespeare, but I knew how to work hard, and I knew how to be true on stage. Chicago Shakespeare really valued strong truth. They had great teachers there who were really in the forefront of the American approach to the First Folio, and they also had a real jazz sensibility about them. That was just the best. Between Chicago Shakespeare and Montana Shakespeare, it was just an amazing experience for someone who wanted to learn. I was really lucky to cut my teeth with them.

Q: WHAT WAS THE EXPERIENCE LIKE IN MONTANA?

A: Montana Shakespeare in the Parks hires anywhere from ten to thirteen young actors, and you do a new play in a different town every night, and you put up and tear down the set – a real Elizabethan sensibility. It's like Joseph Papp/Shakespeare for Cowboys. You fix up your own costume, and if a storm comes up during performance, you hold onto the set. Dogs run on stage, kids run on stage. It's a hell of a place to learn how to speak these words. The artistic director Joel Jahnke took a big risk with me.

I was lucky being able to get comfortable with Shakespeare there, in that environment. But I knew how to listen, and I cared about the theatre. I loved the theatre, and I knew some of these people because I had worked with them in Chicago, and some of them had worked with Mamet and had all this amazing experience at places like Steppenwolf. I stayed in rehearsal all the time instead of going back to the green room. I was just listening, listening, listening. Most of the time, they were very patient with me. I'd take scripts home. The education director of Chicago Shakespeare used to let me sit in the library and just let me watch all these performances of other productions. My learning was apprentice learning.

144

Q: Do you think that was the best type of training?

A: The majority of my training has been simply doing it. I did have some great conservatory training, but I was lucky that I didn't spend too much time intellectualizing it. I tried to spend my time making the work. Just making it, and making it, and making it. I get asked a lot if I'm a professor who teaches drama, or an actor who teaches. I try to just be a theatre professional. I'm lost a lot of the time because I don't really know where I fit. But when I feel lost, I try to make a story and then things usually work out.

I think that's one of the reasons Shakespeare made so much sense. We have a kind of complex relationship to Shakespeare. He's seen as highbrow, and his work is some sort of badge of sophistication. But in his time, his work was accessible to a wide variety of people. He was a storyteller – a Swiss Army knife type of dramatist who used whatever ways he could to reach audiences. That's what I loved about Chicago and Montana – that same approach. Here was Shakespeare, some kid from the country, who just showed up and started making stuff.

Q: You've gained some attention for doing Shakespeare with the homeless. How did that come about?

A: I was really lost, living in Detroit. I went there for my Ph.D. I had been in Chicago for five years, understudying a bunch of roles, and playing the porter in their "Short-Shakespeare" program, which offers Shakespeare to Chicago schools. There were like six or seven of us who had done Montana Shakespeare, and I was also working around the city, trying to write and direct my own plays. I decided to apply to some Ph.D. programs. I got into Wayne State in Detroit, and started teaching right away. I had never been in a city like Detroit. It's difficult to describe if you haven't been there. A young man I was working with on a number of projects got shot in a carjacking. I lost students through violence, had it happening where I lived, right in my building. And I didn't have a car, so I was in that landscape, on foot, exploring it every day. I was feeling like this world didn't really make sense. I remember walking to a grocery store, during a blizzard, and seeing this homeless man talking on the phone, but the phone wasn't connected. He was talking to no one, and I thought about how he's got a totally different reality, and I started thinking about the people in this landscape who were in a different place, a different reality, and had their own stories from this world. And I wanted to explore that.

There was an older bar that was getting rehabbed, and there was a warehouse over it, filled with all this dust and construction equipment, and so I decided to try to do some theatre there. Tell some stories with these people, most of them homeless, and some students, a well as a few people from the community. And they just came out. We found some costumes in dumpsters, and we just did it.

Q: DID YOU HAVE TO GET ANY PERMITS? OR CLEAR IT WITH THE POLICE?

A: In Detroit, it's "no blood, no foul," so nobody really paid attention to us, or told us we couldn't do it. The people at the university weren't quite sure about what I was doing. We played music real loud and after Tigers games, people would walk by and see us, and come up the fire escape and then when we had an audience, we'd do our version of *A Midsummer Night's Dream*.

Q: The full play?

A: What I did is... I really love these plays, but I do some severe things to them. I love the text, but I do believe that Shakespeare had a very living approach to his own plays. Not only was he borrowing from contemporary or historical sources but even in his own plays like *Hamlet*, the actors are adlibbing, inserting their own stuff. We went through the plays, tried to figure out what the bones were, and then put it together in a way that made sense for our time and place. We did *A Midsummer Night's Dream*, but it started out with Puck jumping out of a grocery cart that this homeless man was pushing across the stage. We did all this different kind of stuff, threw in music, and rearranged things to suit our situation. We were just trying to make the best play we could. We read the plays – I love the plays – though we might do great violence to them. I've learned to think of the audience as poets and geniuses. When you treat the audience that way, you can do a lot more. There is a rigor to our method, and audiences seem to get it. I'm not interested in doing it exactly as it's always been done, but many of the tricks we do come from established theatre tradition. The proof is in the pudding. People come, they like, and we learn something about the play. And it doesn't cost anything. If we mess it up, we do it again in a week or so differently.

Q: That's a pretty interesting take. Where do you think your vision of Shakespeare comes from?

A: Growing up, I had a problem with dyslexia, and so the modernized Shakespeare with its regularized spelling didn't really do it for me. But the First Folio, with its odd patterns of spelling, *did* speak to me. I could see the pattern, and it helped me look at the big picture. I could see the bones. It seemed like a theatre maker worked on that folio. I'm not a great playwright, but I willed myself to learn to write. The folio feels like that – he's prompting himself as he goes along, and he invites you to be alive in the text. The folio draws you in in an imaginative way that standardized texts don't. It's like a jazz composition, and you can feel the creation going on as you read. So the spelling and all its other flaws don't matter. That's not what it's about.

Q: ARE YOU INTERESTED IN DOING "TRADITIONAL" SHAKESPEARE?

A: There's a part of me that feels like I am doing traditional. I'm not interested in being controversial, but I am pretty frustrated by what appears to be the norm, or the expected approach to Shakespeare in this country, where directors feel they have to set the plays in an appropriate setting, like putting *Julius Caesar* in the Old West. That's the big idea: that the plays have to be set somewhere. But *Othello* is set in Venice, and there's no talk about boats. The plays live in the imagination of the audience, not in some explicit theatrical setting. I don't need some bullshit civil war framing device for *Henry V*. I love putting actors in suits not because of some commentary about power, but because that's what the actors have. That's a tradition of style based out of necessity. Doing the plays is hard enough – sometimes it seems like a waste of time to put all this effort into tarting the play up. It has very little to do with the play and more to do with the director. I guess I'm lucky to have missed that part of my training. Sometimes it does work, yes, and that's great. But I feel my approach is the traditional one. The play is the thing, but it's not what's down on the page. These are living, breathing texts. Shakespeare's plays are pretty loose, and his approach to other people's plays was even looser.

Q: WHAT ABOUT CONFUSING THE AUDIENCE WITH UNORTHODOX STAGING? IS THAT A WORRY?

A: I'm terrified of that. We just did *Hamlet* [in Ames, Iowa, before a tour of select cities) and took it around. I had this thirteen-by-thirteen pavilion we covered in construction plastic. We had all these hand-made signs in magic marker, like we were a advertising a band. And we wrote the cast list in chalk. We only had six to seven actors, and we told people that some of the characters would be played by suitcases, and we just used what we had, like boom boxes that blasted 80s hair bands. It's not the most traditional approach to *Hamlet*. It might have looked just thrown together, but at the end I think we connected the dots. Sometimes that approach doesn't work, but sometimes it does.

It doesn't work with some equity summer theatres, though. I don't know – sometimes the authentic seems very dangerous to some people. So doing the plays behind a Burger King might seem a little odd, but that's not far off in terms of what Shakespeare was doing. I think we're participating in the spirit of originality. I hope so. I do know I get really frustrated and angry at clichés – it's supposed to be this, it's supposed to be that. The University wits were pretty hard on Shakespeare, but he seemed more interested in breaking the rules, so I think our model works.

# David Neal

***"** It's a fascinating process where you get into a room, and there's a bunch of strangers, and you all go through this process where at the end of the run, you're the tightest of families. It's quite a little arc.**"***

*David Neal, a public relations and marketing professional in Northern New Jersey, made his stage debut as a 10-year-old playing Richard III's nephew in a 1977 production in Ann Arbor, Michigan, where he grew up. He's had a varied career on the boards ever since, performing a variety of roles ranging from Billy Bibbit in* One Flew Over the Cuckoo's Nest *to Menelaus in* Orestes. *His Shakespeare roles have included Touchstone in* As You Like It, *Malvolio in* Twelfth Night, *and Macbeth.*

Q: What was your first encounter with Shakespeare?

A: It was my first Shakespeare role, which I certainly remember. The role was in the biggest building I had ever seen, in a building on the campus of the University of Michigan. The play was *Richard III* – back in Ann Arbor, Summer of '77. There was a notice about the play, and I tried out. Nicholas Pennell [celebrated English actor], he was *Richard III*. He did some selected dates that summer. They needed two kids for the poor nephews. What I

151

don't remember was how I would have seen an audition notice. My mother might have seen it. At the time, I had been doing school shows, library shows, church shows, but I went out for it. One of the most glorious summers I've ever spent.

Q: WHAT DO YOU REMEMBER ABOUT THE SHOW?

A: I was the kid. There was another boy who was a nephew also – but I remember being THE kid in a cast of adults. I remember trying to fit in, trying to be the adult. And I remember succeeding – or at least, in *my* mind, thinking I succeeded. But what I've learned in doing hundred of other shows – when you're in the circle, when you have a script in hand, you're part of it, you're in the show. Everyone is really treated the same.

I can remember they had people doing hair and makeup… and script-wise, I remember that I took the script and separated the pages and put them in the left hand side of a book, like a composition book, and I left the right hand side blank, so I could translate what the lines were. I'm sure I didn't come up with that myself, but it's something I do in some form or fashion with every show I've done since. I do still put my script in those composition-sized books. I just fill it up with stuff. It's mine, not for anyone else to see. Back then, it was "What do I mean when I say this?" Now I write down all kinds of things. There's no room in the margins of a script for those kinds of notes, for digging deep into the text, or your character.

The interesting thing I remember about the show – when it came to tech week, a surprise was sprung on us. Part of the concept of the show was all of us would be on stage throughout the entire show, standing on this elevated structure, easily to the rafters, up 20, 25 feet. All of us non-principals stood as guards as the action was going on. Then we would come on from there, pick up our parts. We didn't do this during rehearsals, just tech week. So I remember trying to stand there for hours, my legs turning to jelly. I remember during the first time we rehearsed this, fainting. I went down in a heap – this is too much for me. Eventually, after the second or third time, I got it. But a ten-year-old kid standing there, all that time, it was too much for me.

Q: ANY OTHER THEATER MEMORIES FROM YOUR SCHOOL YEARS?

A: In ninth grade, we moved to Pittsburgh….at the University of Pittsburgh, they were host to what they called the Three Rivers Shakespeare Festival. It wasn't Joseph Papp's New York Shakespeare Festival, but it was a very good regional Shakespeare fest. We'd do three or four shows in repertory. I was still the kid among adults, but the gap was narrowing. I performed in *Hamlet* there, and *Merry Wives of Windsor*.

Q: WERE YOU ALREADY THINKING OF ACTING AS A CAREER?

A: I loved it! It was fun work for me. I wasn't an athlete, I wasn't a social butterfly. It was something I was relatively good at, and my parents were behind it. My mother had to drive me to rehearsals, wait around, drive me back home…it was really quite a sacrifice. The bug had bitten me, and I would just go from show to show.

Q: DO YOU REMEMBER STUDYING SHAKESPEARE IN SCHOOL?

A: I remember, I don't know if they still call them modules, but we'd have a module in English class: *Catcher in the Rye, Little*

*Women, Shakespeare.* I do think that I felt that I was closer to the material than anyone else. I was the only one in the room doing Shakespeare, here and there. I knew it was different, that it required extra digging, translation. But it was really just storytelling. Up until even the most recent Shakespeare that I did last summer, *Cardenio*, which is a "lost" Shakespeare play, I could not wait! Here was an opportunity to put on a story that I knew ninety-nine percent of the people watching didn't have any idea about, didn't know what it was about. The story was going to be *completely* new to all but the most ardent Shakespeare scholar in the audience. That was so intriguing. Here was a chance to tell a new old story.

Q: DIDN'T THAT MAKE YOUR JOB MORE DIFFICULT?

A: I know it can be difficult to watch – I'm amazed at the number of actors I meet who won't go near Shakespeare. They think it's too daunting. I don't understand that. If you tell the story well, if you build great characters, whether it's Neil Simon or Shakespeare, if you say what you have to say, as an actor, and do your job, the audience will see it. It seems to me that the foundation is the same. In the hands of a good director who appreciates that complexity – and I'm not discounting it – it needn't be an impediment. In his time, the actors who performed Shakespeare didn't have hundreds of years of history, they were just looking to tell a story. And the clues are all in the text. I know it's not for everybody, but I don't understand actors who say "I *can't* do Shakespeare." And I say "*Why* can't you do Shakespeare? You can't sit down, learn what the words mean, and then articulate that. What do you mean you CAN'T?"

Q: How do you balance the rich tradition
of Shakespeare performance — of honoring that
tradition — with the need to keep the performance fresh?

A: I don't think about it at all. It's not that I'm turning my back on history, but for me — and I may be in the minority — when I take an acting job, my job is to deliver the director's interpretation. And I'm a participant in that process. But it is much more for me about what the director wants. So, to the extent that a director is influenced, it might play a part in that.

Q: Do you seek out performances, on film or on stage, of other actors in roles in which you've been cast, to see how they approach the role?

A: I go out of my way NOT to see what someone else did with a role! I'll do that *after* a show, but I will very purposely avoid that while I'm working on a role. I don't think anything good can come of that. An example: I was in *Children of a Lesser God,* and I had the opportunity to see the film. But I didn't. Why? *I've* been cast, and my job is to bring to it what *I* can. But afterwards, sure, I'll take a look at it.

Q: What do you get from your fellow actors?

A: The reason I do this is it's fun work. The reason I fill so many nights with doing this is I love to build a character from scratch, in collaboration with the director and fellow actors on stage. If the very last night that I did a role was the very last rehearsal, I'd be fine with that because my job would be fulfilled. Now, I love performing, applause, all that, don't get me wrong. But if we only made it to the very last dress rehearsal, I'd be fine. That's one reason I do this.

The second reason: I learn stuff every single day I have a rehearsal, but I learn from others – how they interpret the script, how they approach their characters. I learn about what makes me tick, and what makes others tick, by doing shows. It's a fascinating process where you get into a room, don't know anybody, and you're basically naked, and there's a bunch of strangers, and you all go through this process where at the end of the run, you're the tightest of families. It's quite a little arc.

# Sydney Somerfield

**" The plays seem to reflect
what's going on in our
world, whatever's going on
in the world. Depending
on the state of the world
at any given moment,
there's almost always a
Shakespeare play that
comes into vogue because
it reflects the moment. "**

*Sydney Somerfield is an actor and playwright in Portland, Oregon. She holds a bachelor's degree in Theatre Arts from the University of Oregon and is currently in a Feldenkrais practitioner training program.*

*In 2008, she helped found Willamette Shakespeare, a non-profit Shakespeare company with her husband, Daniel. Willamette Shakespeare offers free outdoor theatre in Portland and local vineyards in Willamette Valley wine country.*

Q: Do you remember your first encounter with Shakespeare?

A: We have the Oregon Shakespeare Festival in Ashland, about a five-hour drive from where I live now. They are a professional rep company. When I was nine, my mom took me to see *Cymbeline*, and I still remember it. We got last minute tickets, and my mom picked up a synopsis and we read it before we got there. We sat on folding chairs – they have very nice seating now.

Q: DO YOU REMEMBER READING HIM IN SCHOOL?

A: In high school, the first play we read was *Romeo and Juliet*, my freshman year. Each of us took parts, and we read through the whole play. If we wanted to get extra credit we could do scenes. I remember going to my dad and asking him which scene I should do. And he said Mercutio's death scene is the best scene in the play. So that was my scene. It was fun. I've seen that scene so many times since, and I have a much better sense of what it was about, but back then, the language was a little hard for me to understand. My dad coached me through. A bunch of my friends got together and we got a video recorder and taped some of the scenes. I'm sure I'd laugh if I saw them now!

Q: WERE THE ARTS IMPORTANT AT HOME WHEN YOU WERE GROWING UP?

A: My dad taught journalism, photo-journalism, and then when they cut that department at OSU [Oregon State University], he taught photography in the art department, and my mother has always written – poetry and plays – so art was always a big thing in our house. We had all of the Shakespeare plays, the complete works, on the shelves.

Q: WHEN DID YOU DECIDE YOU WANTED TO BE A PERFORMER?

A: It was probably around my freshman year in high school. I had been thinking about being a veterinarian, or a geologist, but

160

around then they allowed us to do projects in high school, so if we didn't want to do an essay, we could write a play, or perform a scene, and any time I had an opportunity to do a play, I would do it. I think I wrote a play about the death of Rasputin when we were studying Russian History.

Q: DID YOUR HIGH SCHOOL HAVE A DRAMA CLUB? DID YOU JOIN IT?

A: I wasn't really active in the drama club until my senior year. I've always been really shy, so I didn't get involved until my senior year. My freshman and sophomore year, I wasn't able to take any drama electives. I wasn't able to fit it in. Maybe also because my sister was involved, and that was her domain, and I didn't want to get involved. My junior year, I went abroad to Mexico, but the summer before my senior year, I took a drama class as an extra-curricular, and then I got involved in drama. My senior year I did my first Shakespeare show – I was Caliban in *The Tempest.*

Q: THAT'S A PRETTY CHALLENGING ROLE FOR YOUR FIRST SHOT AT SHAKESPEARE.

A: I've been fortunate and unfortunate in that I can be androgynous – I'm tall, and thin, and the boy roles were open to me until I was into college. I didn't play a woman ever on stage until my sophomore or junior year of college. So when they would hold auditions in high school, there would be like three guys that showed up, and then a bunch of these girls, and so we had to divvy up the roles. I *loved* playing Caliban. It was great. I had a friend who wrote some music for the show – that's how into it we were. We would go off and work on lines, try different accents, and I remember coming into one rehearsal and doing all of our lines

161

in operatic style! The director thought that was a really great exercise. It teaches you to use you full vocal range. I just had a great time. I made part of my costume and, weirdly, I started to identify with Caliban. It took me a while to see that he isn't the hero of the play.

Q: IN FACT HE'S KIND OF A BRUTISH CHARACTER, WOULDN'T YOU SAY?

A: I got to come on and growl and yell. I even remember some of the speeches. That was almost twenty-five years ago.

Q: WHEN YOU WENT TO THE UNIVERSITY OF OREGON, DID YOU GO THERE AS A THEATRE MAJOR?

A: I was originally intending to be an English major, but something got messed up with my SATs and I was lumped into the theatre majors. I was going to change it, but the English major line was really, really long and the theatre line had only one person! I went in and got my advising and never looked back. I stayed a theatre major.

Q: LOOKING BACK, WOULD YOU SAY THAT WAS A GOOD EXPERIENCE?

A: Definitely a positive experience, but it was a lot of work. You had your course work, but if you were in a play, you had to coordinate your schedule to work with your scene partners. People get a lot of flak for getting a liberal arts degree, and it shouldn't be that way. You do a LOT of work as a theatre major, and you have to really be good with your time management. If you can't keep to a strict schedule, you won't get work. And you learn to be out in front of people, which for someone like me, who is shy, is very helpful. You learn to put on a persona.

Q: Did you focus in any particular area in the theatre program?

A: If I had a specialty, it was Shakespeare. We did have some musical theatre, but the music department and the theatre department didn't work together very much. Plus, I'm not a singer. I took classes in acting Shakespeare, and I got to be in *Twelfth Night*. We had a student-run theatre, and I was on the board of that. I had a chance to do stage management, and some assistant directing, and I took a directing class.

Q: It sounds like you were preparing for a career in theatre — was that your expectation?

A: I was thinking that I could be an actor, as a profession, but I was also a little nervous. One of the downfalls of the program was they made it really, really competitive, and so I was a little scared to go out for auditions. When I got out in the so-called "real world," I did start auditioning for smaller things, and then I went overseas for about six months – Indonesia – and when I came back I did some auditioning again. I ended up connecting with *The Other Side*, a theatre group here in Portland. They did sort of an edgy style, giving an edge to well-known works, or newer works, and we did a lot of interacting with the audience.

There are a lot of theatres like this in Portland – they take the acting and performance very seriously, but it's not a full-time professional thing. You might get paid for a performance – sometimes you might just split up the proceeds from the show. Beer money for after the show! It was a great way to gain experience. The company was starting to break up, and I moved up to Seattle.

Q: WHY?

A: I really wanted to get into the U of Washington professional actor training program, I wanted to get into residency up there, and my boyfriend was getting into an MFA program. I did apply to that program, and a few others, but I didn't get accepted. I was really disappointed at not getting into any of the programs I applied to – I applied to the top five programs in the United States – but after that, I think I decided that maybe I need to do this as more of a side thing. I thought I could get a job that would earn me a living. I went to massage school, and got a license, and then I moved to L.A. If you want to make it as an actor, that's where you need to go. I still had that desire to act.

Q: HOW DID YOU FIND L.A.?

A: Part of the problem with me and L.A. is I don't drive, and L.A. is not a real friendly place for people who don't drive. New York probably would have been a better choice. I was disappointed to find there wasn't a lot of theatre in L.A. I expected an underground scene, more active. The theatre scene is very different. There are theatres that are like these 99-seat theaters open to actors who are SAG, the Screen Actors Guild. These end up being showcases for certain actors, and it's just not as much fun. So I didn't do too much theatre. Also, I was trying to make a living, and I was doing massage, which requires night work and weekends. It was hard to schedule any theatre work around that schedule. I was there for a year and a half. I decided it would take me ten years to make it as an actor there, so we went back to Portland. Daniel was happy about that – he hated L.A.!

Q: Where did the idea for Willamette Shakespeare come from?

A: It was actually Daniel's idea, though we both love Shakespeare. To tell you how much we love Shakespeare, we incorporated Shakespearean themes into the wedding.

Q: Is Willamette Shakespeare what you envisioned when you started it?

A: I think it's pretty close to what we hoped to build. We're really pretty happy with it. We're making some changes – a lot of the responsibilities have fallen on Daniel, and he works as a software engineer, so he's working really hard. It's a lot of fun, but there's a lot of logistical stuff that goes along with it. We spend a lot of time on the phone, trying to work things out. We've been lucky, though, that we have had such generous donors. But it's been a lot of work. This year we hired an outside director, but we still have a lot of responsibilities.

Q: Such as?

A: Technically, I am the secretary, so I go to the board meetings and take notes. I was more involved when I was assistant directing, or acting. We made a choice this year to pull back a bit – every summer it basically takes over our lives. We've had a few years straight of losing our whole summers. Next year, we're moving to more of a "presenting" model, because there are so many Shakespeare companies in the Portland area. We're going to hire another company to come in and present their show.


Q: WILL YOU MISS THE HANDS-ON INVOLVEMENT?

A: Well, we have other opportunities to do that with the other theatre companies in town. Daniel has some opportunities to direct. We have more opportunities, but it won't be quite as much of the logistic work.


Q: DO YOU MISS PERFORMING?

A: I absolutely miss performing! The last show I did was *Pericles*. There were six of us playing forty roles. It was great. But part of the problem with performing is some actors get in these traps where you're kind of stuck in these sort-of low level jobs where you feel you don't have much of a career, and you have this compulsion to act, and it's difficult. I'm also thinking about going back to school, but that would mean I'm not going to perform for about four more years – can I be away from acting for four years? That's a very hard decision. I think a lot of actors have trouble with that. You have to be available for call if you're performing a show, and your work schedule or school schedule doesn't usually allow that kind of commitment. This is really tough. I've had a lot of tears over this – can I step away from the acting?


Q: IS YOUR HUSBAND URGING YOU ONE WAY OR THE OTHER?

A: No – he knows better. [laughs]

Q: Why do you think Shakespeare is still relevant?

A: That's a big question. A lot of people say this, but he really does have a timeless quality about him. He was really good looking at different sides of an issue, and characters. He rarely presents shallow characters. Instead, you get great characters like Shylock, who is written as a villain, but he's got very human characteristics. There are ways to play that that will make you feel very bad for him, even though he's the villain. Or Caliban. Or Iago. His characters are really human, and his themes are timeless. The plays seem to reflect what's going on in our world, whatever's going on in the world. Depending on the state of the world at any given moment, there's almost always a Shakespeare play that comes into vogue because it reflects the moment.

The other thing is that his language is so amazing. Anytime you get a chance to spend a really concentrated time learning a part in one of his plays, his language just blows you away. He gives you hints about what you are supposed to do with the character. I remember playing Rosalind in *As You Like It*, and her speech patterns are so different from any other character, or from my own, but she just runs along and along – she's a chatterbox, and her speech patterns reflect her character. And the poetry from a play like *Hamlet* – it's just stunning.

# Thomas Cox

> **" I thought if you could act Shakespeare, you could carry that over, act anything else. "**

*Thomas Cox was born in Jersey City, where he attended public schools before entering the New Jersey Institute of Technology. After receiving a master's degree from Columbia University and working there as a researcher, he moved to England, where he lived and worked for many years – and began his amateur acting career after seeing a flyer on a company bulletin board. At the time he had no training or background but loved the experience so much that he took acting classes for two semesters with a British character actor, Ray Roberts.*

*After a few years hiatus he started studying (around 1992) at HB Studio with Geoffrey Owens in his 'Shakespeare Text Analysis' class and quickly became a bardophile. For many years Tom was cast in two or three roles a year only; all non-Equity productions but sometimes with very good casts. Then in January of 2010 he landed the role of King Duncan in the Scottish Play with Hudson Shakespeare and did another four plays with them that year, including playing King Lear. He has also acted with the Oxford Shakespeare Company. He now lives in Ocean Port, New Jersey, and remains active in local theatre.*

Q: WHAT WAS YOUR FIRST ENCOUNTER WITH SHAKESPEARE?

A: My father, who was not a particularly literate man, used to quote Shakespeare at me, even though he knew very little of it. When I had to read Shakespeare in high school, I loved coming across those quotes. But I found it very tough. That was my first encounter – required reading. I loved it, but I was struggling. The play was *Macbeth*, one of the shortest, and probably easiest, to understand. We read *Macbeth*, and *Hamlet*. I got interested, and tried reading him on my own. I decided I would read all of Shakespeare's plays. I attempted to do it. I got through about 10 or 11 plays, and realized that even though I was getting through them, I wasn't understanding all the words on the page, so I gave it up for a while...a long while.

I remember reading a line in *Antony and Cleopatra* that really made me fall in love with Shakespeare. The line has to do with two soldiers discussing the affair between Cleopatra and Julius Caesar. The line is...and this is the entire description: "He plowed her, and she cropped" I said `Oh my God! That is so elegant and concise, and it tells you a lot.' I loved that line.

Q: BUT YOU STAYED INTERESTED IN SHAKESPEARE—

A: Fast forward many years, I'm an engineer. In 1985, we were in London. My company gave me a job over there. Acting was something I thought I'd never want to do, never thought I'd be an actor. I worked for an oil company. The amateur dramatics club of Mobil Oil was putting on a play – on the bulletin board, there was a sheet that said they were looking for an actor. I thought I'd call up the number. Here's why: in my youth, in grammar school, I had several embarrassing incidents in front of class, and they bothered me for several years, eating away at my psyche. I decided I was going to get up in front of a group of people, get this right, learn every word, and maybe that would wipe away these bad memories. The play they were doing was *The Real Inspector Hound.* I played Inspector Hound. It was the perfect play to begin…in the end, you can't tell who the characters really are, they morph into one another. It's a really bad English country house murder mystery – a very funny play. Anyhow, I'm playing Inspector Hound. Because there's no information about these characters, I had to kind of invent who this character is. The play doesn't tell you. Because the role was so crazy, kind of slapstick, I was afraid that if people started to laugh, I'd laugh too. That's bad acting. How am I going to avoid that? I decided that my character is a crazy man, out for revenge, and when the audience laughed at me, I would hark back to my grade school days…the more they laughed, the madder I would get, thinking back to those days, and that would help me focus. And it did! And I fell in love with creating a character in my mind. Who is this guy? Why is he here? Where he is coming from?

Q: WHAT HAPPENED AFTER THAT PLAY? DID YOU STICK WITH ACTING?

A: I decided to sign up for acting classes in London – two semesters of adult education, with an English character actor. He recommended Uta Hagen's book, which says when you enter, you need to know who you are, what you want, where you're going, exactly the kind of stuff I was trying to think about. I fell in love with acting, totally.

Q: As an actor, is there a difference between how you prepare for Shakespeare, and how you prepare for other, more modern playwrights?

A: There's a big difference – but there's only one difference: It takes a lot more work to figure out the text, what you're actually saying, to investigate the words and figure out if they still mean the same as they did then. And then saying the words, as if you were speaking modern language. That's the big difference. In some ways, Shakespeare is easier, because if it's in verse, you know right away if you're missing a word. The iambic pentameter makes memorization easier, I think.

Q: Did you continue performing in London?

A: No, I didn't do anything else with acting after that, and then we moved back here [New Jersey]....I went to HB studio in New York, and after one semester, I noticed there was a guy teaching Shakespeare script analysis, and I said `Wow, that's fantastic!' I thought if you could act Shakespeare, you could carry that over, act anything else. Also, script analysis – you could really explore the plays, understand them. I took his course – a fantastic course. We'd go line by line, word by word, to understand how each line worked in the text. That was fantastic training.

I took courses at HB for years. I was also auditioning. Of course, if you're starting out, and all you have on your resume is Inspector Hound, you don't get too many parts. I was getting one role one year, two rolls the next. Then, it started to pick up, two or three a year, until 2010, when all of a sudden things blew wide open, because of three or four companies I got connected to that seemed to like my work. In January 2010, there was a group that was doing *Macbeth* here, couple of miles away. I auditioned, and it was a terrific production. It was a group called Hudson Shakespeare. I played Duncan, and Old Siward. By this time, I had a lot of training, and I jumped right into it. Apparently, they liked what I did. Next, they did a production of *Taming of the Shrew*, which I was in, and after that they invited me to play Gloucester in *King Lear*. I told them sure, but I wanted to understudy Lear. Something may come up, so I thought I'd like to be an understudy. They said, `Okay.' I said if I do that, you really should give me one or two performances as Lear. Well, what happened was, I went to the first rehearsal, and about ten minutes in, the guy playing Lear had his cell phone go off. He came back in and said to the artistic director that he had another gig and then the director turned to me and said `Thomas, you're in!'

Q: Did you feel prepared to take on that role?

A: About thirteen years ago, when I was still studying at HP, a group started in NYC called *Instant Shakespeare*, started by a guy named Paul Sugarman. He's done staged readings of all of Shakespeare's works every year. I had probably in that series done a staged reading of *Lear* three or four time. Plus in other staged readings I had played Gloucester, Cornwall, Kent....many of the male characters. I had a lot of time working on *Lear*.

Q: What did you think of the production, and specifically of your performance?

A: I think I did well – I heard some great things from some people, and Hudson Shakespeare has continued to cast me since then. Apparently, they thought I was a success. The funny thing is, they say to me that first day, `OK, you're Lear. Tomorrow, we're rehearsing the scene on the Heath' the mad scenes, where he runs into Gloucester. I was confident I could memorize the scene quickly. I worked my ass off for the next twenty-four hours, rehearsing it, going through the scene in my mind over and over. A lot of people on the cast were probably thinking, `Oh my God! We lost our Lear!' Anyway, I went in and did it – completely off book! After that scene, I was walking off the stage and the woman playing Cordelia, whom I had never met, was sitting there, watching, and as I walked off, she gave me a silent `Wow.'

Q: WHEN YOU PERFORM A ROLE LIKE LEAR, WHICH HAS BEEN ACTED BY SOME OF THE GREATEST ACTORS IN THEATRE HISTORY, DO YOU FEEL EXTRA PRESSURE? AND HOW DO YOU KEEP FROM BEING OVERWHELMED BY THE CHALLENGE?

A: All you can think about is the Uta Hagen things: Who's my character? What's his background? You think a lot about relationships, what's gone on before, what's happening now, what's motivating him. Lear acts crazy – what's going on in his head? You focus on that, and not the fact that Ian McKellen and Lawrence Olivier have done it, and done it very well. I tried not to look at any of those performances when I was preparing. I used to think it was so I wouldn't imitate them, unconsciously. But really it was because I didn't want to see them making discoveries. I wanted to discover things on my own.

Q: HOW MUCH OF A CHALLENGE IS IT TO MAKE SHAKESPEARE ACCESSIBLE TO AN AUDIENCE?

A: Well there's no doubt that the audience has trouble following Shakespeare's language, to varying degrees. Because it's Shakespeare, there will always be some people there who know Shakespeare, and can follow it more easily. There's a story of

Richard Burton, who was on stage in London and performing Shakespeare, and he heard this sort of grumbling in the audience, and when he investigated, he found it was Winston Churchill, mumbling the lines along with him. There will always be people like that. But the best we can do is to perform the work as clearly as possible, to speak clearly, focus on word emphasis, inflection, knowing where to stop a thought. You try your best to make it comprehensible. But it's difficult.

Q: WHAT DOES SHAKESPEARE DO THAT MAKES HIM DIFFERENT FROM OTHER PLAYWRIGHTS?

A: The language is beautiful itself. But the thing that struck me about Shakespeare when I started taking the acting classes: his characters are so brilliantly modern in their attitudes and thoughts. I was just really surprised by that – it wasn't just the beautiful language, but the characters really made sense. I love Shakespeare – I love it because, well, it's funny, and though some of his plots are contrived, there's something about his characters and language that really grab me.

Q: ARE THERE OTHER SHAKESPEARE ROLES YOU'D LOVE TO PERFORM? OR ANY DREAM ROLES IN GENERAL YOU'D LIKE TO ACT?

A: It's funny with me, I'm not tremendously literate in terms of theatre. I don't have a long history of going to the theatre, and reading plays. There's a lot of stuff out there I don't know. Dream roles? Yeah – I just got cast in *Inherit the Wind*. Henry Drummond – great role. That's one. In Shakespeare, certainly there are roles. I played Polonius in a shortened version of *Hamlet*. I'd love to do the full play. I'd love to play the Nurse in *Romeo and Juliet*. That could be fun.

Q: WHICH DO YOU PREFER ACTING IN – COMEDY OR TRAGEDY?

A: I love them both – comedy is trickier.

Q: WHAT DO YOU GET FROM PERFORMING?

A: I've thought about this. I'm a fairly shy person. Many actors are. I find that many times, If I'm talking, people aren't listening, But if I'm up on stage, and I'm talking, I'm going to grab your attention. People will watch. Dustin Hoffman once said to Lawrence Olivier, `Why do we do this?' And Olivier said 'Look at me! Look at me! Look at me!' So it allows us to be the center of attention – and also to be inventive, to figure all this stuff out. My original idea twenty years ago to take up something I could do in my retirement has paid off. This has kept me pretty busy – doing something I love. You can't beat that.

# Erin Drevlow Weichel

*" We are so fast-paced, so multi-tasked that we don't even take the time to put words together in a nice stream of thought. You can see it in students, the way they abbreviate everything when texting. They say as little as possible, but Shakespeare was the opposite. He found dozens of ways to say the same thing, each one prettier than the last."*

*Erin Weichel is a midwest native. Born in North Dakota she attended college in Minnesota at Minnesota State University, Mankato. She received a degree in Theatre Performance and a minor in music. While at Mankato she performed as Nora in A Doll's House, Sara Brown in Guys and Dolls, Elizabeth Proctor in Crucible, Bessy in Marvin's Room, and as Betty Blake in Will Roger's Follies. She was a regional Semifinalist (twice) and Finalist in the Irene Ryan Acting Scholarship competition at KCACTF. After collge Erin moved home to Bismarck, ND where she staged and costumed the first full opera in Bismarck since the 1920s.*

*After that she moved to New York City for two years to pursue a career in acting. While there, she was in two national tours with Hampstead Stage Company, a theatre company that specializes in classical literature for children. With Hampstead Stage Company she played numerous roles, including Lady Macbeth, King Arthur, and Robin Hood. While in New York she was also in an Off Off Broadway production of Into the Woods where she played the Baker's Wife. In 2008 she moved home to North Dakota, where she helped create Capitol Shakespeare. Since moving home, Erin's favorite roles have been Catherine in Proof, and Mama Rose in Gypsy.*

Q: Were you always interested in the arts? How did you get involved, specifically, with theatre?

A: I was born in Harvey, North Dakota, which is almost at the geographical center of North America. We were farmers, and North Carolina was going through the farm crisis of the 1980s at that point. And we had lost our barn to a fire, and then we lost our house to a fire...we moved to Wisconsin and rented a farm there. Actually two farms. My dad ran dairy cows, and there was a lot of work involved in running those farms. And my brothers helped. My mom went back to school during that time, and she has a degree in art history and education. And that's when I started getting into the arts. My whole family did, because my mom was an artist, and so the fine arts, and music, were always a part of our life. We moved again to Northern Minnesota, a couple of different places in Minnesota. We ended up in East Grand Forks, and they had a high school that was very active in theatre, so my older siblings got involved, and my mom, because she's an artist, was asked to paint the sets for one of the shows. And I got to go with her and help her. I just kind of carried paint around and cleaned out brushes.

Q: Were you in high school also at that time?

A: No, I was still in elementary school. My siblings were in high school. There are six of us. I'm the fifth of six. And we're all in into the arts – my oldest brother is a visual artist. My sister's an opera singer. I have a brother that also has a music degree. We're all very musical – we used to sing together in church, and for different

180

things around the community. So we were musical and theatrical from a young age. Part of that is my mom being an artist, and part of that is my dad being the son of a pastor, and a very good story-teller, so he was really good at relating to people.

Q: So you grew up in quite a creative household.

A: My mom taught piano so we all learned to read music at a young age. We were all in band and choir. Everybody wanted the Drevlow kids in their band and choir because we came from a musical family.

Q: Given your theatrical background, did you encounter Shakespeare at a young age? Do you remember your first encounter?

A: My first exposure was probably when my sister did something from *The Taming of the Shrew* for a high school show.

Q: How old were you?

A: I was in the fifth grade. But when I was a freshman, we read *Romeo and Juliet*. Our high school's curriculum was really heavy on Shakespeare, so freshman year we read *Romeo and Juliet*, and I had a teacher who been teaching it for years, and he would stop us every couple of lines and explain "this is what this means," and "this is what that means." At first it was a little tedious, but as we got further in that approach made more sense, because then you could start to read it that way on your own and then figure out what the lines mean before he explained because he had done such a good job helping us through it.

Q: THAT'S STILL A CHALLENGE FOR MOST HIGH SCHOOL STUDENTS, I WOULD IMAGINE. DO YOU REMEMBER STRUGGLING WITH THE TEXT, WITH THE LANGUAGE?

A: I really loved it. I didn't find it particularly hard. My family, from a young age we were taught if you didn't know the meaning of a word, you asked, you figured it out, or you found a dictionary. My parents had such a great vocabulary, and they didn't talk down to us. They expected us to come up to their conversation. And so the vocabulary wasn't as challenging to me as it might have been to some of my classmates. And that's a big part of it. And I loved the rhythm of it, because of my musical background. It just all made sense.

Q: DID YOU GET INVOLVED IN THEATRE IN HIGH SCHOOL?

A: I did. I got involved in musical theatre. I didn't do any Shakespeare until I got to college, but I read a lot, and helped students study it in high school.

Q: TELL ME ABOUT THE MUSICAL THEATRE ROLES YOU DID.

A: In high school, I did Maria in *West Side Story*. Then the other plays I did nobody knows. They were plays my director wrote. But then I did *Little Women* at a community theatre. And then I went to a community college for a year [Bismarck State College] and I did a show there. I was originally going to be an English teacher, because I loved literature, and that's where I ran into a college professor who pretty much became my mentor and he said "I think you should consider acting." So I did. I transferred to the University of Minnesota –Mankato. I did a lot of shows there.

Q: Do you remember taking any Shakespeare courses in college?

A: I took a Theatre History course that touched on Shakespeare. And I remember we read *Hamlet,* and I had a bunch of friends who didn't get it. So I said I'll help you out. I thought it would be like two or three people, but there ended up being like twelve or fifteen people, and even some graduate students. I was kind of intimidated by that, but we talked a lot about what words mean, what they mean in particular use in the play. And that got me into analyzing Shakespeare from a literary sense, and how to dissect the play.

Q: So you immersed yourself in college in Shakespeare's language, his plays. And you got a degree in theatre?

A: Theatre performance. And a minor in music.

Q: What happened after you graduated?

A: I went home for a year. My father had a small stroke and so I was home, and then I ended up coming out to New York City. I had never been there before.

Q: What were you thinking?

A: I was going to be an actress...I was going to be star on Broadway! That's what I was thinking. And I had no idea how to do that, but that's what I was going to do. I moved here and I was really homesick, being 1,600 miles away from home. I lived in Williamsburg, Brooklyn – a sublet from a friend of a friend of a friend sort of thing. And I lived there for a month. One of my roommates came home one night and had an extra ticket for Shakespeare in the Park so I said "Okay – let's go." It was the closing performance of *Mother Courage and her Children*, with Meryl Streep and Kevin Kline. I got to see both of them on stage. I was homesick until that moment. Then I said "This is what I want to do." That performance blew me away – it changed my perspective on theatre.

So then I did some auditions, and I got a job with a touring company that performs classical literature for kids. They're based out of New Hampshire – they're called Hampstead Stage Company, and I toured with them for like a spring semester, and then I went back and worked with them again. I also did some stuff in the city between those tours. But that was really amazing – we did, like, *Macbeth* for kindergartners, you know, Shakespeare for Elementary School kids. And you'd think they might not get it, but they understand it – they know, they can figure it out. That was wonderful to work on. The second time I toured with them I went from New Hampshire to North Dakota and back. That was a long tour – but it was really fun.

Q: WHAT HAPPENED AFTER THAT?

A: During rehearsals of that second tour, I got a phone call. We were up in New Hampshire – the phone reception was really awful – and I got phone call from my family, and I finally got a hold of my mom, who said my dad had had a massive stroke. We didn't know if he was going to make it through the night. They got him stabilized. He had been away on business, but they brought him home.

I had been planning to go home that summer. I just needed a break from touring. So I went back home in May of 2008 and I've been in Bismarck ever since.

Q: Things seem to be going well for you in Bismarck.

A: Yeah, it's true. I think that's really where I was meant to be. I love New York, loved being there, but when you're not Equity, it's really hard to get work, so I feel I'm being of more use to theatre and the acting community here than I ever was there. In Bismarck, there was a theatre company that had been started that summer I came home. There were three young ladies who had gotten together. They all loved Renaissance fairs and they thought North Dakota needed to have one as well. I ended up directing *Twelfth Night*, thinking I was just going to do it that one year. And then I realized I wasn't going to leave for sometime, so I became artistic director.

Q: Willingly?

A: I willingly took the directing role, and then I fell in love with the idea of a Shakespeare company in North Dakota. I saw how many people came to it. I decided it needed to continue. My family life was really hard at that time because my dad was so sick, and this was something that gave me a feeling of accomplishment, and that I wasn't just there to take care of my dad.

Q: HOW DID YOU FIND THE ACTORS FOR THAT FIRST PLAY, SINCE THERE WASN'T A LOCAL TRADITION OF SHAKESPEAREAN PERFORMANCE?

A: There's a really well established community theatre in Bismarck, and we contacted them. And I contacted a number of my friends who I thought might be interested. One of my dear friends came and played the role of Sir Andrew Aguecheek. He was studying opera, and he asked if he could sing some of the part, and I said, "Go for it."

Q: YOUR FIRST YEAR WAS A SUCCESS?

A: Yeah, we learned a lot. Afternoon shows outside are a bad idea! We learned you have to move the shows to a different part of the capitol grounds so the audience is more protected. I learned a lot about how to cut Shakespeare. The first time you do it, you think "I've cut enough," and then you watch it and say, "No, I didn't." But the thing that was great was the amount of support we got, people coming up to us saying, "That was great!" and "I hope you'll do it again." Then the following year we did *Merchant of Venice*, which is my favorite Shakespeare play. It was nerve-wracking because it was my favorite.

Q: HAS THERE EVER BEEN ANY TALK ABOUT EXPANDING THE NUMBER OF SHOWS YOU DO?

A: Yep, there has been. The problem with that is finding a home base, because in Bismarck, you can't perform outside year round.

Q: You've spent a lot of time thinking about Shakespeare — what is it about him? Why, four centuries later, are people still lining up to see his works?

A: We don't think like that anymore. We are so fast-paced, so multi-tasked that we don't even take the time to put words together in a nice stream of thought. You can see it in students, the way they abbreviate everything when texting. They say as little as possible, but Shakespeare was the opposite. He found dozens of ways to say the same thing, each one prettier than the last. Kids think it's wordy at first, and they don't want to get into it, but I tell them it's like a foreign language. After a while, it will just make sense if they keep up with it. There's such a beauty in the way he puts things together. Plus, the stories relate to all of us — these stories have been around forever, about greed, about love, about power, and he tells these stories so well.

Q: Are you an activist director? Do you give a lot of direction, or do you cast the play and let the actors go their own way?

A: I'm really active, but I don't give line readings, because I want the actor to figure it out himself or herself. But sometimes I'll tell them to check the stress on the line, check the pronouns, look at the versification. Usually then an actor will figure it out. And I'm always walking around the stage, checking the blocking, looking at it from the audience perspective. And I try with characters, especially with the fool, or a servant, I try to work in a lot of intense physical stuff, because it's funny — it's supposed to be — and that little kid sitting there watching will then be able to get it to. The parents laugh at the joke, and the kid laughs at the physical stuff. It's the Pixar version of Shakespeare.

Q: Are there any Shakespearean directors or actors who have influenced you and your approach to Shakespeare?

A: When I first got into Shakespeare, Kenneth Branagh was really starting to get things moving with all his adaptations. In high school, we watched his *Hamlet.* I thought it was phenomenal. I've tried to watch all his work. He's very committed and dedicated to what he does, in all his roles. He also understands the play is a living thing, and it can be interpreted so many different ways, and that's okay. I've always been impressed by his work.

Q: What do you say to people who come to you and want to be in your show but have little or no experience, and they might be intimidated by the material? How can you ease their fears?

A: Well, that's usually about fifty percent of my cast. I usually have a sonnet to give them, and I say "Read this – don't worry about the meaning, just say the words." I want to hear how they engage with the language. And then I'll put some of my more experienced actors in the room, and we'll do a scene, and they can see where an actor comes from, and how they play with a scene.

Q: If you had the resources and cast to do any Shakespeare play, which one would you do?

A: Well, actually the one we're doing this summer [2013] – *The Tempest.* North Dakota is very proud of our pioneer heritage. I would love to do the play and set it in the time of the settling of the prairie. And *Prospero* is a native American Chief who has been left there by his family as they moved on – I think our audience would have a stronger understanding of that than setting the play on a tropical island. We're very landlocked in North Dakota.

# Matthew Van Gessel

> **"** *Even in a soliloquy, you're trying to communicate an idea to someone else: to God, to the audience, to someone.* **"**

*Matthew Van Gessel is an acting student at the North Carolina School of the Arts in Winston Salem, North Carolina. A native of Westport, Connecticut, he has been acting all his life, taking classes at the Music Theatre of Connecticut and playing leading roles in plays throughout middle school and high school. His Shakespeare experience began in sixth grade when he saw a local production of A Midsummer Night's Dream. Since then he has been hooked, having acted in Romeo and Juliet, Hamlet, Midsummer Night's Dream, A Merchant of Venice, Much Ado About Nothing and Twelfth Night. He as also directed Hamlet and Macbeth with fellow students of acting.*

Q: WHAT'S YOUR FIRST MEMORY OF SHAKESPEARE?

A: Very, very first? Obviously, the name floated around. I had heard Shakespeare's name, and I knew he was a writer. In about fifth grade, I remember seeing, I think it was Anthony Hopkins, *Titus Andronicus*...I was pretty young to see that movie. I think I remember getting it from my pubic library for the simple reason that the front of the DVD box looked interesting. I thought, hey, I'll watch this. I was mostly initially taken in by the visuals. I thought all Shakespeare must be like this. I dug a little bit deeper. I think we read *Much Ado About Nothing* in sixth grade. Westport [Connecticut] schools are pretty highly rated. It was a very early introduction to Shakespeare. For some reason, the language of Shakespeare, I liked it. It didn't strike me as being as difficult as it sometimes strikes others. But I also loved the puzzle-solving aspect of reading Shakespeare. I remember acting scenes out in school, not being restrained by the verse. I would read until I came to a period, acting it more than reading it as poetry.

Q: YOU WERE AN ACTOR, EVEN THEN?

A: I was interested in acting and theatre prior to even starting school. When I was a little kid, I loved music and theatre. I was taking after-school classes in play-acting when I was in kindergarten and first grade.

In elementary school, one of the defining moments of my life: there was an Egypt play and I was NOT cast in it. I was baffled. I was one of the few kids who was really into theatre. It made me wonder if I was as good as I thought I was. I think that has motivated me still.

Q: WHAT ARE YOUR OTHER MEMORIES OF SHAKESPEARE IN
SCHOOL?

A: In middle school, we read *A Midsummer Night's Dream*. I had
pretty much been turned on to Shakespeare by the stuff Kenneth
Branagh does, putting Shakespeare in different time periods or
places. The other plays I was reading were filled with stage directions, but in Shakespeare, the most description you usually get is
"Exit the King" or "They fight." He boiled it down to all you need.
I like the idea of the freedom to go and just perform it.

So my freshman year of high school, already into Shakespeare – I
had seen some movies, and a few community theatre productions.
I really liked the movie of Kevin Kline in *A Midsummer Night's
Dream*. My freshman year, we did *Romeo and Juliet*. I was Sampson,
and one of my best friends was Gregory. The director had come
from Carnegie Mellon…The idea of this *Romeo and Juliet* – all
the costumes were in black and white. And Romeo was this off-
white blue-y color, and she was this off-white pinkish color. The
idea was that it was taking place in all time periods simultaneously.
You'd have someone listening to an ipod and then you'd have a
sword fight. The idea is that the theme of the play is timeless, that
Shakespeare himself transcends time. That's something I was really turned on to. I thought: Wow, I could take *Hamlet* and set it
in the present, explore all of these things in my own work with
Shakespeare

Q: HOW DO YOU PREPARE FOR A ROLE?

A: It all depends on the role, and the amount of time you have.
Right now, I'm doing *Whose Afraid of Virginia Woolf?* I'm playing
George. The first thing I'll do is read the play in one sitting, try-
ing to read the play in the amount of time it would take to watch

the play. Then, I'll continue to read the play, over and over. You keep finding stuff on the sixth, seventh readings. But first, I take it easy, just try to read it through, starting to think about how to get a handle on it. Then, generally, I research. I make sure I understand the meanings of all the words, the references. I break it down like an English class would do, looking closely at scenes, trying to find the central moment of each scene. Then I do the same thing for the whole play.

Q: IS THAT YOUR APPROACH TO SHAKESPEARE AS WELL?

A: I would especially be researching Shakespeare. The most recent Shakespeare I did was *Merchant of Venice*. I played Lorenzo. I took the same approach – started thinking about the whole play before focusing on my part, trying to explore the play in general, looking for essential information. Then I try to think of a spine for the play...in terms of acting, you always need to be doing something, or trying to fulfill a need. Acting isn't just being, it's *doing*, so I try to find the spine of the play.

Q: SPINE?

A: The reason I use that word: it's the central armature of the human body, and it's that way with a play too. You have to find the core idea, though it changes as you constantly work on the play, going deeper. Really what's important about that, once I make a spine for the play I can work on my character. The important thing about the character spine is that will inform all the choices I make about the character. If I'm unsure, I can return to that spine and work on stuff like beats and actions. I give an active verb to each line. With this line, I want to "annihilate." With this next line, I

194

want to "console." I've even consulted the thesaurus to find these kinds of verbs.

Q: How'd you come up with this approach?

A: It has to do with the reason I chose this school. There are lots of different acting methods: Stanislavsky, Meisner, Uta Hagen…. but this school tries to teach all of it. So I go to all these classes, gather up all these tools, and then I have all these tools in my box. So it's something I've constructed myself out of the things I've learned in class. There's a lot I've learned that works for other people, but not for me.

Q: What do you hope to do with all these tools?

A: I'm looking to make it as a professional actor and director. Preferably as an actor who directs. I've also done some writing. In high school, I used to be pretty passionate about film. I audit film classes, and I also assistant direct, so I can learn from the directors I'm working with. I really want to act for a while, then end up directing, and I'm trying now to learn all that I can.

Q: Do you see a difference, in terms of what one gets out of Shakespeare, between acting the text and simply reading it?

A: Obviously, it depends on the person. I think the experience is pretty similar. If I read something that is emotional, and it's really good, I'm moved by it. If you are really actively reading Shakespeare, I see it almost like the same thing. When I'm feeling down occasionally, I'll read *Hamlet*. It's so cathartic. If you read Shakespeare with the intent of really getting something out of it, you can really connect. Acting just requires you to make some choices, read between the lines. An actor needs to read between the lines, but as a reader, you can let the emotions and words just take you way.

Q: ARE THERE ANY PARTICULAR SHAKESPEAREAN ROLES YOU'D LOVE TO PERFORM?

A: Hamlet, I'm sure, will top most actors' lists, men and even women. He's got pretty much some of the best lines ever. I just think it's the best play ever written. I can't think of a single flaw. He's such a deep character, I'd love to sink my teeth into that role. Bottom in *A Midsummer Night's Dream*. Petruchio [in *The Taming of the Shrew*], he's funny, and flamboyant. And Mercutio in *Romeo and Juliet*. I've see Mercutio many, many times, but I feel like there are some things missing in the performances I've seen. That's the fun of Shakespeare – you can play things so many different ways.

Q: WHAT HAVE YOU LEARNED FROM WATCHING OTHER ACTORS' INTERPRETATIONS?

A: Generally, when I watch anything, if I like something, I need to figure out why. I don't get when people say "I like it," and you say "What did you like about it?" and they say "I don't know. I just liked it, but I don't know why." I need to break it down.

When I'm on stage with other actors, when I'm really doing it, I don't think about it in terms of being an actor, but rather a character. Generally, what I'll learn during a scene is how to just give your self over to something. It's about connecting with an acting partner. But even in a soliloquy, you're trying to communicate an idea to someone else: to God, to the audience, to someone. When I'm on stage acting, everything I want needs to be in my partner's eyes. They are the person I need to communicate with, and when you have an honest connection with someone, it's palpable. That's when acting really moves me. You get that sixth sense: they *are* that character.

# Lynn Petko

> **"** I would have been an actor, gone into theatre, if I had known I was going to love it this much. No doubt. **"**

*Lynn Petko lives in Brownsville, Pennsylvania and is a senior instructor at Penn State-Fayette, where she has taught English for more than twenty years. She is the advisor to a student group on campus called the `Lion Players' – a group of non-theatre majors who perform Shakespeare. She also performs with the group, as well as teaching the popular "Stage to Page" course, which culminates in a full production of Shakespeare. She is one of the founders and principal script writers for the `Nitwittany Players,' a group of local performers comprised of Lion Players alumni.*

Q: When did you first encounter Shakespeare?

A: I remember reading him in high school, but the first play that really got me going with Shakespeare was *A Midsummer Night's Dream,* down at Pitt, performed outside. It might have been the first live Shakespeare I'd ever seen. I was just blown away. It was after I graduated high school. I went to Pitt for a year before coming back to Brownsville. It was an evening performance. I was struck by how different it was to see a live play, not just to read it. Watching it outside, there was this open stage, the actors flitting back and forth. It was like fairies were coming out all around you.

When I went to Pitt, the idea was to go to medical school. Looking back, I think that was more my mom and dad's idea. It was such a competitive, cutthroat major, it kind of turned me off... I had taken psychology, and I came back with the thought that I'd get a psychology major. But I've always loved English. I got my degree from Cal [California State College, in Pennsylvania]. My undergrad degree is secondary ed/English.

Q: DID YOU ORIGINATE THE "PAGE TO STAGE" COURSE AT PENN STATE- FAYETTE?

A: Denny [Prof. Dennis Brestensky] started it. I got involved the second year, as assistant advisor. I've been doing Page to Stage for probably about five to six years. Page to Stage students are, for the most part, Lion Players.

Q: DO YOU REMEMBER WHAT THE FIRST PRODUCTION YOU GOT INVOLVED WITH WAS?

A: The very first play we did was *A Midsummer Night's Dream.* I loved it from the beginning. The time involvement – the time you put in is crazy, but I loved it. I can't imagine not doing it now, or not putting those hours in. I think I'm closer to the students now then when we first started. It seems that once someone becomes a Lion Player, they are always a Lion Player. I kept wanting to start my own acting troupe of Lion Players, people who went through the troupe....getting plays together and presenting them, taking them around to schools. We decided a couple years ago we were going to start doing things outside of the Lion Players.

Q: That's the Nitwittany players, right? How did that start?

A: My husband John found this contest – a four-minute contest that had certain specifics you had to satisfy. You had to start with a red screen, someone had to die, it ended with a red screen. So John came up with it, he wrote a little script. I took it, tore it apart, and said let's do this and this. And then Chris, Stephen, Paula, and Cynthia [former students and Lion Players] came over, read it, and we figured out how we wanted to do it. We filmed it, it was 90 degrees at midnight, it was crazy. That was our start into it. From there, we did a little thing we helped two students who were in a film adaptation of Shakespeare class. The Nitwittany players were the background people for that production. So that was our second thing we did. I wanted to do something all our own, something really funny, so we made *Hamlet II: Grave Secrets*. We filmed it, and my husband is now editing it.

We met almost every Sunday, sometimes Saturdays, depending on schedules. We met from May until July to do "Grave Secrets." Once we get it done, we'll send it around to contests.

Q: Since Penn State-Fayette doesn't offer a theatre major, do you have a hard time finding students for the Lion Players??

A: Some of the kids have done acting before, but some never have. It seems like a lot of our kids are looking for a place to be, a home base. They want to attach themselves to something.

We have, across the road, a residential building called "the commons." Those kids, for the past couple of years, I'll make sure they get involved. There's a girl from Africa, a boy from Columbia, we get a lot of students who aren't really attached, they don't have a place to go. We try to include them all – our current play, we have about six of the commons kids in the current production..

Q: DO YOU HAVE A BACKGROUND IN THEATRE, OR IN SHAKESPEARE?

A: I took Shakespeare in grad school, and then took Dr. B's [Dennis Brestensky] Shakespeare class... so I know about Shakespeare. I never had any formal training with the acting. I think I'm just a ham. If I would have stayed at Pitt, I think I would have found my way on to the stage. I would have been an actor, gone into theatre, if I had known I was going to love it this much. No doubt.

I don't really ever find being on stage terrifying. I love being on stage. As long as I'm playing funny roles, I'm fairly good and comfortable. Sometime I have a bit of trouble learning long chunks of lines. But I love being the comic character.

I've never performed outside the Lion Players. I have been Nick Bottom, I played Touchstone, I played one of the witches in *Macbeth*, I played the Porter, the grave digger. I was Mistress Quickly.

Q: DO YOU EVER PLAY "SERIOUS" ROLES?

A: I have one this year. We're doing *Romeo and Juliet*. I really wanted to play the Nurse, but I have to defer to students. So my role is Lord Capulet. That will be me yelling and screaming at Lord Tybalt, and throwing Juliet all over the place, and yelling at the nurse. People might not know how to react, seeing me in a non-comic role. They're in for a surprise.

Q: DO YOU PERFORM THE FULL PLAYS, OR DO YOU DO ABRIDGMENTS?

A: Denny would never let us cut anything – we did *Love's Labors Lost,* and we couldn't even cut the Latin scenes! We had to find a way to make them work. We had over five hundred people last year. We got a great reaction – I think they liked it, and we work really hard to make sure the audience knows what's happening. If necessary, we occasionally modernize, update the words a bit. You have to have the audience with you.

Q: WHAT DO YOU LIKE ABOUT PERFORMING?

A: The feeling I get when I'm on stage is like nothing you can get any other way. To make people laugh, and to make them understand what's on the page…it's so special with Shakespeare. I've taught other classes where we just read plays, but Shakespeare is special. You can use so much of yourself in any role you take on. That's not true with all playwrights, but it is with Shakespeare. I love to go out there on stage and become these characters.

Q: WHAT DO YOUR STUDENTS GET FROM PERFORMING SHAKESPEARE?

A: Oh, I think they grow. I think they become so mature from what they're taking on, from the sort of power they create, what they can create for an audience. I think it makes them feel good about themselves, like they can achieve so much more. If I can do this on stage, I can find that job I want, run that company I'd like to start. I think they find confidence, and they develop great friendships from it.

Q: OKAY, THE PERFORMANCES ARE FUN, BUT WHAT ABOUT THE ADMINISTRATIVE TASKS OF MOUNTING A SHOW WITHOUT A THEATRE DEPARTMENT TO ASSIST YOU?

A: I have to be on top of getting all our rehearsal dates. If it's on the big stage, I have to make sure things are cleared. We're not always their number one priority. We get money through student affairs. They know how hard we work, how much we bring in, how many people come to the shows. Usually, we can even give them some money back. I wrote a grant in the spring for travel money, and got some money from the Alumni Association, and we took some students to University Park [Penn State's Main Campus] and saw *Sweeney Todd*. It was wonderful – some of our students never had been to that campus. There were about 33 of us. Some of those kids were never even in an art museum. It was overwhelming. We went to some of their acting classes. It was a great day all around.

Q: HOW DOES IT FEEL KNOWING YOU'RE HAVING THAT KIND OF AN IMPACT ON STUDENTS – MAYBE EVEN CHANGING THEIR LIVES?

A: That feels wonderful - to know you are having that kind of an effect. You have to have that feeling if you're working that hard with so many students, and the inevitable conflicts and chaos that comes up. But when it all works right, then it helps calm me down. It makes me feel like maybe I wasn't supposed to go into acting. Maybe I was supposed to be right here.

# Michael Callahan

*" Shakespeare tells great stories about the things that remain constant among us. That's really what makes him great."*

*Michael Callahan, a retired computer programmer, has been an active member of Lompoc Civic Theatre in California since 2001. He has performed as writer, actor, director and stagehand in various productions for main-stage, dinner theatre, and special events. He has had minor roles in two Shakespeare productions, A Midsummer Night's Dream, and Twelfth night. The most difficult part for him was trying to memorize lines when he couldn't understand what he was saying.*

Q: You got involved in theatre after you retired. Why?

A: I had never really done any acting except in high school – though I did some writing. I wrote a novel, which was unpublished. But after I retired [in January 2002], I was looking around, and I saw that a local theatre was looking for people.

Q: GIVEN YOUR LACK OF THEATRE EXPERIENCE, WERE YOU AT
ALL RELUCTANT TO JUMP IN?

A: It was more or less spontaneous – but in my career, I was
involved in Toastmasters. I also got invited by some friends – got
interested in stand up comedy. I got comfortable going in front of
audiences, performing these little skits I wrote. But I never really
had an ambition to be an actor. I found that I'm a little bit of a
ham – it was fun going up on stage, but I had no ambition to make
a career out of it.

Q: WHAT ROLE DID YOU AUDITION FOR?

A: Well, the first thing I did was open and close the curtain.
Then they were short a few people, and they asked me, "Why don't
you audition for us?" That happens a lot, I've discovered. People
often get sort of drafted into the theatre. So they said "Read for a
part." I don't think I got it. But I've had several parts since, some
pretty big parts. It's been fun. My first part was in dinner-theatre,
a play called *Shopping could be murder*.... A year after that, I wrote a
play called *A Town Meeting*. That's what got me interested in play
writing – I've written several since, and got some of them produced. I've really become interested in the 10-minute play.

Q: DO YOU REMEMBER WHEN YOU FIRST ENCOUNTERED
SHAKESPEARE?

A: High school. I can remember it quite well. We were doing
Shakespeare, junior year. We'd use the lines of Shakespeare in
kind of a silly way among ourselves. We didn't actually do a play in

school, we just read the plays. I had never been in a Shakespeare play until fairly recently. That was *A Midsummer Night's Dream* – I had a very small part in that. I had a speaking part, but it was one of those things – just a few lines – I can't even remember what they were.

My other Shakespeare role was in *Twelfth Night*. I was the servant. My entire speech was [here he recites ten lines from the play] :

"So please my lord, I might not be admitted/But from her handmaid do return this answer/The element itself till seven years' heat/Shall not behold her face at ample view/But like a cloistress she will veiled walk/And water once a day her chamber round/With eye-offending brine – all this to season/A brother's dead love which she would keep fresh/And lasting in her sad remembrance."

Now, I didn't understand one word of that! Even when I knew what it meant, memorizing that was agony for me. And I've memorized pages and pages of dialogue. This terrified me, when I would do these few lines.

It helped a little when I finally figured out what was going on. One of the other things that helped was, we were rehearsing in a local high school, and the drama teacher had a comic book of the play, and it's funny, because that was really helpful….I was in there bitching about Shakespeare, about how tough the language was, how incomprehensible, and she said "This might help you," and she handed me a comic book of the play. They have the lines, and then they have an explanation of what they mean. She said "Here's what I give my students. This might help." And it did.

Q: How much time did you spend trying to learn those lines?

A: Well, the director, who had just graduated about a year ago – came back to our group, and he'd always wanted to direct a Shakespeare play. This was his idea, the thing he did that was different. We have a schedule of plays we do each year – but this was something he wanted to do…so he just came up with this unusual idea: *Twelfth Night*, in twelve days! That's all we had to rehearse. But because we only had twelve days, the actors were allowed to use their scripts if they needed them. But I memorized my lines, and I was very impressed that most of the actors with parts much longer than mine also memorized their lines.

Q: Did the shortness of time make it even more difficult to work through the play?

A: Well, it wasn't so much the time, but the thing I feel awkward about with Shakespeare is, when I get into a part, I try to be real. I like a part where I can let my emotions out, and really understand the feelings. That's tougher with Shakespeare. Of course, I was only playing a butler in *Twelfth Night*. I might feel differently about getting into character if I were playing Hamlet [laughs].

Q: Even having a small part, did you feel somehow connected to, or a part of, centuries of theatre history?

A: I'm not a big theatre traditionalist. I don't get awed by being in a Shakespeare play – though I realized after I took a trip to the Globe Theatre what a big part of our culture he is.

Q: Are there other Shakespeare parts you'd like to play? Any dream roles?

A: Not at all. I found it so tough with just those lines. But, I suppose if somebody asked me to be involved, I think I'd say yes. But I'm not looking for it. I'm not even reading Shakespeare. I had a couple of friends who saw *Twelfth Night* and they said "Hey, you were good!" That's enough. I'll take that.

Q: Do you have any thoughts on why Shakespeare remains so popular today?

A: Great question. I've thought a little about it. I think because the plays were written for the people. They were popular shows, written for an audience. And I think he just did it so well – conflict, action, humor, all the talents he possessed. Like most people, I like a good performance. Shakespeare tells great stories about the things that remain constant among us. That's what makes him great.

# Tony Pisculli

> **"** *When you work on a Shakespeare production, you own it. Shakespeare is the sort of author who is very much worth making that investment of time.* **"**

*Tony Pisculli is the co-founder and producer of the Hawaii Shakespeare Festival, which recently completed the canon in its twelfth season. He directs one of the three plays each season. Highlights include biannual all-female productions of such plays as Two Gentlemen of Verona, Henry V and Richard III, a gender-blind production of Timon of Athens (co-directed with Eleanor Svaton) and an all-male production of Merry Wives of Windsor. He has received Po'okela awards for Excellence in Directing for the Henry VI trilogy (an edited version of all three plays in one evening), Merry Wives of Windsor, Henry IV, Part 2 and Richard III. He is also a fight director and has been teaching and directing stage combat in Hawaii for 20 years. He has received multiple Po'okela awards for fight choreography and is a Master Instructor with Dueling Arts International.*

Q: WHAT WAS YOUR FIRST ENCOUNTER WITH SHAKESPEARE?

A: I think that my first positive encounter with Shakespeare was a production of *Rosencrantz and Guildenstern Are Dead*. That was an amazing play. It was a family trip, and we drove to the boonies to see it. It was one of the first plays I had seen. It was outdoors, and we didn't get to see the whole thing. It started raining, and I remember the footlights exploded. It was just a remarkable play. I was right at that age where something like that could have a real impact. I was about 16. There weren't a lot of opportunities to see plays in my town. After that, I started to read plays.

Q: WERE THERE A LOT OF BOOKS IN YOUR HOME?

A: My parents were avid readers. It was ridiculous. There were books in every room, floor to ceiling in a lot of rooms. So I read some plays, and then I read more plays in college. [UC Santa Barbara] My next encounter with Shakespeare was probably in the standard English comp class. I think we read *Hamlet.*

Q: AFTER THAT?

A: I went off to the Seattle area, Redmond, Washington, for five years to work for Microsoft. I couldn't handle the weather, so I moved to Hawaii. I was looking around for something to do. I took some classes at the time, classes in Physics, took some computer classes. But I was pretty bored with that...more of the same. Sitting around in Hawaii in a cinder block building, surrounded by computer guys. I looked through the course catalog, and looked for something different, completely different. I saw an acting class. The idea of acting scared the crap out of me. I thought it would be a challenge. The thought of being on stage scared me.

Q: HOW DID THE CLASS GO?

A: We had a great teacher, Megan Evans. It was a summer class, met every day, low key, no pressure. It was just a lot of fun. Not a lot of "OK, you're a tree." Or, "Now cry!" It was more about, "Let's just play. Let's have some fun." A lot of improv, a lot of games. It was a very gentle introduction. I really enjoyed the class, and I wanted to do as much as possible, right away. There was nothing offered for the second session, not for six weeks. So I took a speech class, and I haunted the department, looking for acting opportunities. I ended up doing an evening of futurist dramas. The plays were all about two minutes long. One was an adaptation of a massive five-act play reduced to five lines! The other was just a diagram. Strange stuff. I was in about 13 of these sketches.

Q: WHAT WAS THAT LIKE?

A: It was interesting…I was and I wasn't terrified. One of these plays had a nude part – the statue of David. That's not something I'd jump at today, but coming off these classes, which were such a rush, that was something I was willing to try.

Q: SO THEN YOU WERE HOOKED?

A: I just wanted to do more of it. The next thing played a big part. That fall semester, I took Acting II, and another directing student told me I should audition for a work she was doing and I was really flattered, so I said sure – not knowing she was asking every guy in the class to audition. But there was also an audition for a Shakespeare play – this was back in 1993. *The Merry Wives of Windsor.* I went to that audition, got cast, and also got cast in the other play. It turns out there was a conflict between the two plays. Because the Shakespeare director was a professor and the other a grad student, I took the Shakespeare play! I was Master Abraham Slender.

That was amazing. To be part of that rehearsal process, to sit there and watch other people, talented people, really work at it, was terrific. There was a sense of ownership of the play that I never would have gotten from reading the work. I really felt it belonged to me. So yeah, I had the acting bug, big time. I went on to do about twenty plays or scenes over the next few years. I did everything I could – main stage, late night, readings, any thing I could. And then I finally decided acting wasn't for me as much as directing.

Q: WHY DIRECTING?

A: I'm much more of an analytical person. I had a realization that I was never going to be a great actor. There's an aspect to me, even though I'm comfortable on stage, there's a reluctance to be vulnerable in the way that actors are. There was always, always this part of me that I was holding in reserve. This is my analysis in hindsight. I'd see somebody on stage letting their soul spill onto the stage, and I'd say, I can't do that. I'd have directors push me in that direction, but I'd say "That was as far as I can go."

Q: WAS THE ADJUSTMENT FROM ACTING TO DIRECTING DIFFICULT?

A: I would say I had a great deal of confidence, but not a great deal of competence. I was still just taking classes, I was nonmatriculated, non-baccalaureate, so the directing classes were off limits to me, but I wheedled my way into them. And I ended up getting into the program.

I could make all the decisions as director, but I was no longer responsible for the emotional content. I was much more comfortable behind the scenes. I was still performing improv, which I did for about ten years. But I was doing it in this very clever, witty way – not the same demands as genuine acting.

Q: What about Shakespeare? We're you interested in directing his works, or had you moved into other areas of interest?

A: After *Merry Wives of Windsor,* I had a number of encounters with Shakespeare. A couple of grad students started doing Shakespeare outside on the lawn, a zero-budget, pass the hat kind of deal. I did two of those, and they were a lot of fun. A friend of mine, who ended up co-founding the Shakespeare fest, did *Macbeth* and *A Comedy of Errors.* I was the assistant director for *Comedy of Errors.* I learned a tremendous amount working on that production. Assistant director is one of the best jobs you can have in the theatre, because you have the ability to have a tremendous amount of creative input without the responsibility of putting the show together. You can just sort of sit back and say "I think we could try it this way." I didn't have the responsibility of scheduling rehearsals and all the production details. I just got to sit back and play.

So *Comedy of Errors* was the same summer as the final production of Shakespeare on the Lawn. The people running it handed it off, and I directed the next outdoor production, *Love's Labour's*

*Lost* – it was my first time directing a full play. I had responsibility for everything: casting, finding the performance space, costumes, everything. We found some incredible people, many of them from *Comedy of Errors*.

So it's my first production, and my lead dropped shortly after being cast, and a few of her friends dropped then as well, and I thought, "Oh no. This is the end of it, my first directing assignment!" But we just shuffled some folks around, and I performed in it as well, since we didn't have enough people to play all the parts. Some friends saw it, some people from the university. They liked it.

Q: IS THAT HOW YOU GET INVOLVED WITH HAWAII SHAKESPEARE FESTIVAL?

A: The fest started in 2002. R. Kevin Garcia Doyle and Harry Wong were temporaries at the University of Hawaii, and they did their MFAs the same time as each other. I think R. Kevin said "We should do a Shakespeare fest this summer." There was a new theatre opening up, and he said "We should do three plays, and each of us direct one." My reaction was "That would be awesome!" At the time, it was just supposed to be a one-off, Summer Shakespeare. I went into this thinking "Hey, were gonna scrape up five hundred bucks apiece, and put this thing on in t-shirts." They said, "No, no no no...we need to have sets, lights, and costume designers," and I'm wondering where we're gonna get the money for this. I think we estimated we could make about $20,000 over a six-week run. I had some money, and I said, well, if we are going to make it back, I can front the money. That's not quite how it worked out. We had a good run, made a splash in the local theatre scene, but we didn't make the money back. But that's how I got to be the producer.

Over the course of twelve years, there's been a familiar pattern of "Oh my god! The Shakespeare Fest is coming up!" We've got to put everything on hold. Chaos, having to put our lives on hold, asking "Why are we doing this?" – and then when it's over, saying "Can't wait to do this again!"

Q: WHAT IS THE APPEAL OF SHAKESPEARE TO AUDIENCES TODAY – AND TO YOU AS A DIRECTOR?

A: Those are very different questions. Obviously, one of the appeals of Shakespeare is that he's Shakespeare. He's a known quantity. You can't go wrong seeing Shakespeare You *know* you are going to see something good. Because he's so prominent, you're seeing something that has been re-mixed, reinterpreted, put out there in so many ways that when you go to see him, it seems very familiar. You've heard all these quotes from the plays. The stories in Shakespeare are amazing. Then you layer on everything else he does so well: theatricality, language, and the universal stories he tells.

Q: HAS DIRECTING THE PLAYS CHANGED THE WAY YOU READ SHAKESPEARE?

A: After all this time, I don't really enjoy reading Shakespeare myself. That's my least favorite part of preparing for the plays we do. I loathe it. But part of what we do as directors is we make sure we're very, very clear in understanding the story, and communicating that to the audience. That requires the actors to be very, very clear in their intentions.

We have a wild mix of skill levels in the Shakespeare Festival. We have professional actors perform with us. We have people who have never been on stage before perform for us. That makes for a really great experience. That makes it really dynamic. There are very few people who will audition for a play who don't want to give it their all. Nobody comes in and says " Hey, I'm just going to audition and then half-ass it." They really want to be a part of this. And it's my job as director to help them give everything they've got.

Q: YOU'VE ESTABLISHED A TRADITION OF CASTING WOMEN IN MEN'S PARTS — IN FACT, OF EVEN HAVING ALL FEMALE CASTS. WHAT'S BEHIND THAT?

A: The tradition has been – let me back up. My very first production was an all-female *Two Gentlemen of Verona*. Some people think I must have a political reason. But it's much more pragmatic. We were doing three plays, and we had to cast all these plays. We had more than 100 people show up, and more than half were women. If we had cast according to traditional gender roles, we would have been casting every man that walks through the door, but only the top five or six talented women. What an incredible waste of talent!

I anticipated, frankly, a lot more artistic obstacles than there were. The casts were great to work with. The one thing was that people didn't really expect it. People were like "Wow – You've got women playing men's parts." Honestly, I felt at first like I had to justify these all-female concepts, and I worked out this whole vision, these concepts where the idea is the world of these plays contains only women, and they'll have to play the men's roles. I was working on the play *Henry V*, and constructed this sort of elaborate idea about women and war, and I just dropped it, and it was a relief because it just wasn't necessary. I had a talented cast and they just happened to be women, and they were playing these roles.

Q: Do you prefer to work with the same actors each production, or with unknowns?

A: Both. But it's much easier to work with someone you've worked with before. I sometimes like to cast actors who I know will bring something particular to a role, and then I can take chances with other actors, see what they can bring.

Q: You've directed other works besides Shakespeare's. How does that compare?

A: This spring, I just directed *The Belle's Stratagem*, a non-Shakespeare play. I was fortunate to see a brilliant production of that show at the Southwark Playhouse, and I was just blown away. It was a brilliant production. I committed to directing it before I had actually gone back and read the script. And then I discovered the script is a mess! The director of the London show had done some brilliant interpretation, cutting and changing the script as needed. But we made it work.

I've also produced and directed some of my own stuff. One of the things I always felt – even if you know you want to be an actor and nothing else, it will help you so much to be a director, even just to look at the auditioning process from the other side. And as a playwright, to put words on a page, you have to imagine how they will be spoken. It's incredibly valuable for actors, directors, and playwrights to try out each of those roles.

Q: What would you say is your strength as a director?

A: I've been having this conversation with some of my actors. You're going to get a different response depending on the actor.

With stronger actors, I try not to be prescriptive. I try to give them leeway to develop the character, rather than say "Stand there and read the line this way."

Q: AS A DIRECTOR, HAVE YOU AND AN ACTOR EVER HAD IRRECONCILABLE DIFFERENCES?

A: That's pretty rare. If I have an idea, I might ask an actor to try it out and we'll see if it works. If an actor isn't comfortable, if it doesn't work, then we'll try it another way. I did lose an actor once – we just fundamentally did not see eye to eye on the character. So she left the show.

Q: DO YOU THINK IT'S A GOOD IDEA TO WATCH OTHER PERFORMANCES OF SHAKESPEARE PLAYS WHEN YOU'RE PREPARING A PRODUCTION? DO YOU ENCOURAGE YOUR ACTORS TO DO SO?

A: I think it's a distraction. If you are playing Richard II, and you go see Ian McKellen's production, you're not going to be doing yourself any favors. It's an impossible measuring stick. Plus, that was *that* production, and this is *our* production.

Q: WHAT HAVE YOU GOTTEN FROM PERFORMING/DIRECTING? HAS IT CHANGED YOU IN SOME WAY?

A: I don't know if it has changed me. It's given me a passion to pursue. I was really drifting before I stumbled onto theatre. When you work on a Shakespeare production, you own it. Shakespeare is the sort of author who is very much worth making that investment of time. I've directed twelve, fourteen of his plays. Those are works

I feel I have a deep knowledge of – much more than if I had just taken a class.

And it's given me a role in the community. I get to be one of the Shakespeare guys. That's nice.

# Michael Hagins

**" I could have easily gone for a different degree and gone after higher paying jobs. But I choose this. I choose having less money. I choose the struggle because I love doing theatre. "**

*Michael Hagins is the artistic director of C.A.G.E. Theatre Company. He won the 2013 Best Playwriting Award in Planet Connections Theatre Festivity for Hit and Match, and is an award-nominated Fight Director/ Choreographer. In addition, he has directed over 40 Shakespearean productions, including Two Gentlemen of Verona: A Swashbuckling Comedy! for the 17th Annual New York International Fringe Festival, and acted in over 100 such performances.*

Q: Do you remember your first encounter with Shakespeare?

A: I remember when I was eight years old I saw *Othello*. It was at a theater in Florida. My parents took me to see it because they knew how much I loved Shakespeare as a kid. I read a lot when I was a child.

Q: THAT'S PRETTY EARLY TO BE AN ESTABLISHED FAN OF
SHAKESPEARE — EIGHT YEARS OLD.

A: We had these encyclopedias when I was growing up, and I
used to just read them, and I remember reading this whole section
that was dedicated to him, so then I read some of the plays, and
I enjoyed them. So my parents took me to see it, and I really enjoyed it, loved the language. I liked theatre, seeing people get up
on the stage and act. That just always felt comfortable to me. And I
remember very clearly that Othello, the actor playing Othello, was
like this statuesque guy, had this wavy hair. Had to be six foot six.
And Iago was like this short guy, barely five nine, balding. And the
dynamics were amazing. Even though Othello could break him in
half, Iago had him, like, crying on the floor. I remember that most
vividly. I can see it now, right now, in front of me.

Q: SO THIS EIGHT-YEAR-OLD SEES *OTHELLO* — DID YOU COME
AWAY SAYING "WOW, SHAKESPEARE'S GREAT!" DID IT MAKE YOU
WANT TO SEE MORE PLAYS — OR WANT TO ACT?

A: All three. The thing that struck me was just the play format.
I actually started writing plays after that. I remember a play I wrote
called "The Boy Who Hated Christmas." The premise was this kid
who is always getting picked on, so he doesn't feel like giving out
gifts. And the presents he always got were lame. It wasn't a very
long play. Basically, it was like *A Christmas Carol*, where the boy
builds a time machine and goes back in time to meet Ebenezer
Scrooge.

Q: USUALLY WHEN A YOUNG PERSON HAS A LOVE FOR ART, IT
SOMETIMES IS A RESULT OF HIS UPBRINGING. IN THE HOUSEHOLD

YOU GREW UP IN, WAS THERE A LOT OF EXPOSURE TO ART? BOOKS?
MOVIES? MUSIC?

A: Lots of books. My mother was a teacher. My father was a cor-
rectional guard, and he was in the Air Force, and so there was a lot
of discipline in the house. But it wasn't like it was rigid. They were
just very smart, and they wanted me to be educated. So I read a lot
of books. I watched TV as well, but I found myself mostly reading
books.

Q: SO THAT WAS ELEMENTARY SCHOOL. YOU'RE WRITING PLAYS,
READING SHAKESPEARE. WHAT WAS YOUR NEXT SIGNIFICANT OR
MEMORABLE THEATRICAL EXPERIENCE? WERE YOU IN PLAYS IN HIGH
SCHOOL?

A: Throughout middle school, there was no drama. So when
I got to high school, I played football for about a year. But then I
tore up my knee in the last game of the season – tore my ACL. And
then that led me to being in drama, because, well, what else was I
going to do with my time? So in a way, the injury was good, because
it got me into theatre. And I realized how much I loved doing it.

Q: WHAT KIND OF A THEATRE PROGRAM DID YOUR HIGH SCHOOL
HAVE?

A: Well, it was "under-funded" – that's the best word I can
think of to describe it. The theater itself was at the elementary
school, which was in the city limits. The high school was outside
the city limits, like a few miles away. So if we were in the theater, we could only rehearse at night, or we'd have to rehearse
like in the high school cafeteria, and then move all of our stuff

over to the elementary school for the performance. It was very disjointed. No one seemed to really care after my sophomore year. Freshman year was pretty good, because the teacher seemed to really care about theatre. The second year she was there, we had a great time with the festivals and whatnot, but then she got another job, and the person they brought in was an English teacher who was there because she had free time on her hands, and drama just sort of disappeared.

Q: IN TALKING TO OTHER ACTORS, I'VE DISCOVERED THAT THEIR PASSION FOR THEATRE CAN OFTEN BE TRACED TO A PARTICULAR TEACHER, AND SCHOOLS THAT HAVE EVEN A SHOESTRING BUDGET FOR DRAMA, IF THE DIRECTOR CARES, THE KIDS ALSO CARE. BUT THE OPPOSITE CAN ALSO BE TRUE.

A: Well, yes, and for me, I never really got inspired in high school because I never really felt like I completely fit in. I never fit in with the drama club because they were kind of clichéd, off in their own little world. And I was like a football jock who got good grades, and I loved theatre, and I guess I didn't fit the image of the typical black person, and therefore I didn't feel connected to any one group. I felt kind of disconnected from everybody. But when I was onstage, I felt good. I mean, it felt more complete. When I graduated from high school, I wanted to go into a drama program. I didn't want to be a lawyer, or a doctor, or an accountant. I wanted to be in theatre.

Q: DO YOU REMEMBER ANY SPECIFIC EXPERIENCES IN THE CLASSROOM THAT INVOLVED SHAKESPEARE? ANY PLAYS YOU MIGHT

HAVE READ? ANY CLASSES WHERE YOU HAD TO MEMORIZE A SONNET, OR A LINE FROM THE PLAYS?

A: Shakespeare? No. Honestly, we didn't really do much Shakespeare. We learned about it, but there was never any time that we like opened the plays and read the lines. Looking back, that disappointed me a lot. There were plenty of opportunities to do that. Maybe they thought kids just wouldn't be that interested in it. The drama club never did any Shakespeare plays.

Q: BUT YET YOU PERSISTED IN YOUR INTEREST IN DRAMA. AND YOU WENT TO COLLEGE AS A DRAMA MAJOR?

A: I was an honor student in high school, I never failed a class, always had good grades, and my guidance counselor was like, "OK, what do you want to be? Do you want to go to FSU? Or the University of Florida?" And I was like, "No, I want to go to a conservatory and study acting." And he was like, "What?

I got a scholarship to go to Florida School of the Arts, full ride, everything paid for, even the books were paid for, and I spent two years there in that program.

Q: WHAT WAS THAT EXPERIENCE LIKE?

A: I enjoyed it. I had a teacher there named Patricia Crotty. That was my inspirational teacher. She was the one who really introduced me to doing Shakespeare, from *Much Ado About Nothing*, to *Love's Labour's Lost*, to *Romeo and Juliet, Othello, Hamlet*. She loved

Shakespeare, and it was obvious. Taking her classes, you could tell she had a real passion for doing Shakespeare, but she was also realistic. She would tell us "You're not going to make a lot of money doing this. It's a passion thing." And I was okay with that. But she was the one who inspired me to keep going with it.

Q: AND YOU GRADUATED FROM FLORIDA SCHOOL OF THE ARTS?

A: I did – with a degree in Acting. And then I went two more years to get my bachelor's degree at Florida Atlantic University. Now, in my four years of college, I never played a lead role. Ever. I would audition for the main stage shows they would have, but I was never good enough to get a lead role. I was always either the servant, or the lawyer.

Q: YOU SAY YOU WERE NEVER "GOOD ENOUGH"...DO YOU THINK THERE COULD HAVE BEEN OTHER FACTORS INVOLVED IN THOSE CASTING DECISIONS?

A: I would say 75% of it was my voice, because I talked really fast, and I stuttered more than I do now. It took me ten years...

Q: PARDON MY INTERRUPTION, BUT I HAVEN'T NOTICED YOU STUTTER AT ALL SINCE WE STARTED THIS INTERVIEW.

A: I know. That's because I really work on it. I still do sometimes when I get nervous, or I get like a million thoughts in my head. It comes out kind of weird. It took me a long time to get rid of all that. I worked on it every single day. It's hard because I have a mix of accents in my head, from Brooklyn to southern, from Florida to Georgia, my parents were from the south but I was raised with a sort of northern mentality. Everything clashes in my head sometimes.

Q: CAN THAT BE AN ADVANTAGE TO YOU AS AN ACTOR?

A: Yes and no. When you have to do accents, it's awesome. I'm good at learning them, at picking them up. But the bad part is, when I have to use just my normal voice, I have to work extra hard just to be clear on stage. I'm doing *Titus Andonicus* right now. I'm Aaron. And the big challenge is just to make sure the audience will understand me. If they don't understand me, then they won't like me, and my character kind of loses the whole point.

Q: THE WHOLE TIME YOU WERE IN SCHOOL, DID YOU ENVISION MAKING YOUR LIVING AS AN ACTOR? OR DID YOU THINK THAT FAR AHEAD?

A: I thought a little bit ahead. I wanted to be successful in theatre, and success for me wasn't being rich, or established as a movie star. It was just living a normal life doing theatre. Sort of the Broadway actor type of lifestyle. And maybe teaching. I just wanted to be in the theatre. I realized early on that I was making a sacrifice. I could have easily gone for a different degree and gone after higher paying jobs. But I choose this. I choose having less money. I choose the struggle because I love doing theatre. I have been in situations where I chose a show over not being able to pay my rent because I love theatre so much. Nowadays, I don't act as much. I direct, I write, I produce. Acting has kind of been put on the back burner because I've gotten to do most of what I wanted to do in acting. I still love it, but I'm not twenty anymore. And it's getting harder to memorize lines. Now I'm like, "Why doesn't that stick in my head?"

Q: SO AFTER YOU GRADUATED WITH A BACHELOR'S DEGREE, YOU CAME TO NEW YORK TO MAKE IT AS AN ACTOR?

A: For two months, I was just temping, different jobs, being a bike messenger. Admin assistant. Typical minimum wage jobs in the city. My rent was $125 a week, which is not that much, so I was able to afford it. I mainly focused on auditioning. I auditioned four times a week, on average. I just went for everything. The first show I got into was a Shakespeare show – *A Midsummer Night's Dream* as Tom Snout, in Red Bank, New Jersey. It was a non-paying show, and I paid thirteen bucks, roundtrip, to get there and back, after work, at rush hour, twice a week. Never once did I regret any of that. It was a lot of fun – I loved it. It was a two-week run, a little theater in the round. It was great because it was my first show, my parents came to see it, and they really loved what I did with it. It was a beginning. When that was done I auditioned for more stuff, and I got a national tour starting in December. I had to move to Virginia for six months.

Q: WHAT WAS THE SHOW?

A: It was a show called "Buffalo Soldiers," by a company called *Theatre IV*, a touring company that also did kids' shows. It was about soldiers in the Spanish American war, about black soldiers having rights and everything, you know, having equality in the armed forces. It was six months, and I traveled as far west as

Denver, and as far north as Canada, and south to Florida, and we even came to New York, to do a show in the Hamptons. It was a fun six months. And I made some money, which helped me a lot when I got back.


Q: So you were getting paying gigs as an actor. Did you think "Hey, I've finally made it."

A: Well, from 2001 to about 2010, I never stopped working. I was doing a show consistently. If a show was closing, another was opening, or we were rehearsing. I never had a break.


Q: We're you able to support yourself as an actor?

A: I was still temping. Every show I was in rehearsed at night, so I was doing temp work. But I had some long-term jobs. I worked at Viacom for three years. I was doing pretty well. I always knew though it wasn't quite enough. I was doing shows, but not really shows that were seen. I was doing shows in Brooklyn, in Long Island, in Staten Island. I only got a couple of reviews, but nothing that was going to take me to the next level. I auditioned for the occasional independent film, and I got a few things. Nothing really big, just some short films. But theatre was the main thing.


Q: In that decade, between 2001 and 2010, we're you doing any directing?

A: I started directing in 2004.

Q: WAS THAT A CONSCIOUS CHOICE — OR WERE YOU JUST THROWN INTO IT?

A: Thrown into it. I was at the Impact Theatre in Brooklyn, and the theatre director, he lost a director for a show, and he asked if I directed. I had done a few things in college, and he said I want you to direct, give you a chance to get some experience. He said "You can do *A Midsummer Night's Dream.*" And I was like "Really?" and he said "Yes, it's perfect for you, do it." So I did it. I cast it, I directed it, and it was a great show.

Q: WHAT DID YOU DISCOVER ABOUT YOURSELF AS A DIRECTOR DURING THAT SHOW? WAS THAT AN ANXIETY-INDUCING EXPERIENCE, OR DID YOU FEEL PRETTY COMFORTABLE.

A: I felt comfortable in spots. My ideas worked. People liked my ideas, but my execution left a little bit to be desired. But I was new at it. I tried to maintain authority but also let people have some freedom, a little bit of leeway with their characters. I had a lot to learn, but I enjoyed it. In acting, you create one character and that's it. In directing, you create all the characters, and you make them fit into your vision of the show. And it seemed to work out well. And also, I built a theatre company from the ground up. The guy who played Bottom in the show, we combined our resources and started a theatre in Park Slope, Brooklyn for about nine months. I directed *Twelfth Night*, directed *King Lear, Love's Labour's Lost,* and that experience taught me a lot. The great thing was, I was doing shows I knew. I had either been in them, or I studied them like crazy.

Q: WHAT WAS THE NAME OF THE THEATRE COMPANY?

A: Waterloo Bridge Theatre Company.

Q: AND IT LASTED FOR ABOUT A YEAR?

A: Almost. The theatre producer, my partner in all of this, he stole money and ran off to India. When *King Lear* was over – the show made about $1,600. The show closed on a Sunday. I left the money in a cash box, as I always did, and I locked it up. Monday morning I came in, cash box was gone.

Q: HOW WELL DID YOU KNOW THIS GUY BEFORE THIS HAPPENED?

A: We were great friends! We hung out all the time, we had conversations. I thought we were friends. Next thing I know, the rent's not paid, his stuff is gone, and he's disappeared.

Q: HAVE YOU EVER HAD CONTACT WITH HIM SINCE THEN?

A: No.

Q: WHAT'S THE PRIMARY CHALLENGE OF MAKING A GO OF IT, AS A NEW THEATRE COMPANY?

A: Money. It's always the money. You can get people to see your shows. There's no problem building shows, no problem creating shows, no problem even getting people to be in them, or getting an audience. The problem is the capital, just keeping the theatre going. If you don't have the capital to pay the rent, you won't last. And by capital, I mean you've got to have the start-up money there, and enough to keep it going. You can make money with your shows, but when that money runs out, you've got to have capital to keep it going.

Q: YOU'VE CARVED OUT A NICHE FOR YOURSELF AS A FIGHT CHOREOGRAPHER. ARE THERE MANY PEOPLE IN THE THEATRE WORLD WHO HAVE THAT SKILL? I WOULD THINK THAT MOST SHAKESPEARE COMPANIES WOULD BE IN NEED OF THAT KIND OF INSTRUCTION. AND YET IT DOES SEEM TO BE A RATHER ARCANE SPECIALTY.

A: There are lots of people who can do combat. You give them a sword and they can figure out how to use it. They can even do the choreography of a fight. But very few can use stage combat to tell a story. If you can tell a story with your fight scenes, you make the show a better overall show. Very few people can do that.

Q: WHEN YOU DO FIGHT CHOREOGRAPHY THEN, DO YOU FEEL YOU NEED TO UNDERSTAND THE CHARACTER BEFORE YOU CAN GIVE HIM OR HER DIRECTION?

A: One thing I put into my fights: every character has a signature: what they do, what they like. Take Macbeth: He's big on flashing his might, being stronger than his opponent, like when he faces Macduff. So you need to build a fight based on who's doing the fighting. People are different, physically. And a character might be injured, or have some other sort of physical trait. Every character fights differently, and you've got to teach them from the beginning what the fight is, what it says, and then have them move according to that. The fighting can tell a story, and it should be part of the overall direction of the play.

# Peter Howell

*" The performing and literary arts have enriched my life immeasurably, partially by offering insights into the human condition, and partially by offering escape into other people's stories, which are generally more interesting and more revealing of the human condition than my own. "*

*Pete Howell's theatrical career (such as it is) began when he was in high school, with roles as Creon in Antigone and Boxer in Animal Farm. Fast forward several decades to the first decade of the current century, when he was drafted to play the Judge in Twelve Angry Men at the last minute. Since then, he's played a variety of supporting roles, including Bogart in Play It Again, Sam and Charlie in Death of a Salesman.*

*He has spent much more time on the dark side of the footlights. Along the way, he worked for about 15 years as arts & entertainment editor of two different newspapers. As such, he was the ex officio theater critic.*

*Pete has also been active behind the scenes. In 2008, he co-wrote the script for the Habitat Follies, and served as stage manager. He completed the Tred Avon Players' Director Training Workshop in 2008, and their Stage Management Workshop in 2014. He directed Play Ball! for the Tred Avon Players in 2008, a staged reading of Twelfth Night for the*

*Historical Society of Talbot County in 2009, and a full production of Twelfth Night for Shore Shakespeare, which he co-founded in 2013. He coached the Easton Middle School Drama Club and directed two plays, 2000 and 2001.*

Q: DO YOU REMEMBER YOUR FIRST ENCOUNTER WITH SHAKESPEARE?

A: My first encounter was probably reading *Macbeth* in high school. I thought that it was surprisingly full of blood and guts, and that, you know, for something that was hundreds of years old, and was required reading, it wasn't bad. I think I was a junior when I read it.

Q: HAD YOU EVER SEEN SHAKESPEARE ON STAGE, OR ON TV OR THE MOVIES, BEFORE THAT?

A: I'm sure I had never seen a Shakespeare play performed. I think I was probably expecting something kind of boring because it was centuries old, and I was required to read it at school. That's not a fair prejudice, but probably a fairly common one.

Q: WHEN DID YOU START PERFORMING?

A: My high school had a drama club, and I had a bit part in *Liliom*, which *Carousel* was based on. And then we did a radio play of George Orwell's *Animal Farm*, and we also prepared and rehearsed but never actually presented *Antigone*.

Q: Why not?

A: I have no idea. Might not have had room for it on the school calendar, or perhaps the speech teacher didn't think we were ready. I didn't perform again until adulthood.

Q: Do you remember encountering Shakespeare after that first time, with *Macbeth*?

A: I did go to college for a couple of years, and read Shakespeare while there…wait, I think I read *Hamlet* when I was a senior in high school. I have no particular recollection of that, except that I think I may have had the idea that everybody dies.

Q: Most high school students don't get into Shakespeare. Why do you think that is? Are they just too young?

A: I think it might be a good idea for high schools to present Shakespeare more often than they do, because he plays every bit as well as he reads – maybe better. And around here at least, the community theatres are reluctant to present Shakespeare. If high schools presented it, there'd be more to see, and those students, when they grow up, might be more amenable to performing it.

Q: How did you get involved with Shore Shakespeare?

A: I'm a retired newspaperman, and was the arts and entertainment editor for the local paper, and the de facto theatre reviewer, so

I got to know lots of people in the theatre community. A director of the show *Twelve Angry Men* approached me to get involved when he had someone drop out, and I stayed involved with generally small roles, and I enjoyed them. Hanging around with show folk, I sort of kept my hand in performing. I have a protégé of mine at the paper who had a hand in working with a theatre troupe, and every so often when they needed someone with grey hairs, they called me up.

Q: What were some of your favorite roles?

A: I enjoyed playing Bogart in *Play it Again, Sam,* and I played Charley in *Death of a Salesman.* I had several small roles in various productions of *A Christmas Carol,* which is always played every year, somewhere.

Q: What was your first Shakespeare experience on stage, and how did that come about?

A: My wife is the president of the local historical society, and four years ago, one of their people had the idea to do a production of *Twelfth Night,* ON Twelfth Night [January 5]. We did a staged reading, and it was fun, and I thought "This is great."

One of my problems with community theatre is it takes so long to get a show ready, and by the time you're ready to go on, I'm sick of it. But with a staged reading, you're in, you're on. My friend Chris Rogers contacted me and said he and Avra Sullivan had been talking for the longest time about why none of the local troupes would do Shakespeare, and they decided to do it, and they had a director lined up for *Twelfth Night* but something happened. They said, "We lost our director!" and asked me if I knew anybody who could direct this show. So I gave them a couple of names, and told them I had been part of a staged reading, and then they called back in a couple of weeks and said, "Can you direct?" and I said "Why Not?" I have a weakness for saying yes when people ask me for things.

Q: Did the experience of the staged reading make your decision easier?

A: Well, I did have some familiarity with the play….I'd like to say I picked the players, but as you know, in community theatre, you can only pick the people who show up, and we didn't have a large turnout. But everybody who showed up was used.

The ability level was pretty good, from high school students to a fellow who had had years of experience with a now defunct troupe called Shakespeare on Wheels, presenting Shakespeare throughout Maryland. He was our Malvolio – and he was excellent. Some of the cast had some experience doing Shakespeare, and others had theatre experience but not much Shakespeare.

Q: Did it help your cast that you had some experience as a Shakespearean?

A: I wouldn't consider myself a Shakespearean. I have never performed in a Shakespeare play – I don't know that I would want to. The memorization would be challenging.

Q: HOW INVOLVED WERE YOU AS A DIRECTOR?

A: My approach was laissez faire. I prefer to let actors find the characters for themselves. If they start to go astray, I might say something. But I find it's easiest for the actor if the director allows them to find their way. It's also easier for me. I don't want to suggest I abdicated my directorial responsibility. Like everybody who reads the script, I take something away. But I don't have a specific template in mind that I try to squeeze everybody into.

Shakespeare was an absentee playwright when it came to stage directions, so I added an awful lot of blocking and stage directions. And I went through the plays very closely with a glossary, and I annotated the script so that the actors would know what they were saying. And occasionally, I'd put in something like "says angrily" or "smacks forehead while speaking," but mostly it was just for the actors' benefit, to help their understanding.

Q: WHY DON'T MORE COMMUNITY THEATRES PERFORM SHAKESPEARE? IS IT BECAUSE OF THE CHALLENGE OF MAKING SURE THE ACTORS UNDERSTAND THE LANGUAGE?

A: I think it's because they feel audiences might have a hard time understanding Shakespeare fully. But I don't think it's necessary for an audience to understand it fully. The corollary to thinking it will be hard to understand is that it will be a hard sell. They think they can get a bigger audience for *The Music Man.*

Q: Did your *Twelfth Night* draw an audience?

A: We did three shows, and by local standards, we did okay. We had a total audience for the first two performances of over 200, and a total audience for the third show of 130 people. The first two performances were ticketed – we were doing the show in conjunction with a local arboretum, and it was a fundraiser for them. The third performance was at a town park in Chestertown, Maryland, and it was free.

The feedback was very positive, and I take that with a grain of salt. No one comes up to you after a show and says "Man, that sucks," But people will often say nice things, which they did.

Q: We're you happy with the show?

A: I thought our first two performances were great. I thought our third performance was lacking a bit. I'd give it a B-minus. There was a lag between performances of the shows, and we had to do some re-casting for the third show. But we are here to stay. There will be additional shows. Right now, we're in the process of forming a selection committee, and they'll consider directors for the next show, as well as the show itself. I suppose when you're trying to bring Shakespeare to the masses, a comedy is easier to sell.

Q: Do you want to continue directing?

A: I wouldn't mind, but I'm just a guy off the street. We have a four-person steering committee, and one of my concerns is that we don't become corporate in our thinking. I prefer a seat-of-the-pants approach.

Q: If they needed performers, would you act in a Shakespeare play?

A: Yes, I will probably audition in the future, but my lack of interest stems from three things: don't like having to learn lines; don't like wearing makeup; and until recently, I was rather large and didn't feel comfortable being on stage.

Q: What do you think is the reason for Shakespeare's continuing appeal?

A: I do believe his work is timeless, and I think that part of the reason for that is he explored universal themes. And he was a clever wordsmith, though much of that cleverness is often lost on twentieth-century audiences – which doesn't mean they shouldn't be exposed to it. He did such a good job of constructing plots and creating memorable characters and exploring themes. I believe those are the factors that have made his art every bit as relevant today as it was in his time.

Q: What would you say you've gotten from your experiences with Shore Shakespeare, in particular – and from the arts in general?

A: Well, the performing and literary arts have enriched my life immeasurably, partially by offering insights into the human condition, and partially by offering escape into other people's stories, which are generally more interesting and more revealing of the

246

human condition than my own. To say nothing of having given me the opportunity to have gotten friendly with a number of creative and really wonderful people.

I think the arts have been kind of dumbed down in recent decades for an audience that is increasingly uneducated and unsophisticated. And I guess that's one reason I like Shakespeare, and what he still gives audiences. Doing Shakespeare offers a unique opportunity for the people who are involved – not just for the audience, but for the performers, the crew…it offers a unique experience, and I am grateful to be able to be a part of that.

Made in the USA
Lexington, KY
27 June 2014